The Secret and Power of
Praying
the Lord's Prayer

SARAH KERUBO NYANDORO

ISBN 979-8-88540-875-2 (paperback)
ISBN 979-8-88540-876-9 (digital)

Copyright © 2022 by Sarah Kerubo Nyandoro

All rights reserved. No part of this publication may be reproduced, distributed, or transmitted in any form or by any means, including photocopying, recording, or other electronic or mechanical methods without the prior written permission of the publisher. For permission requests, solicit the publisher via the address below.

Christian Faith Publishing
832 Park Avenue
Meadville, PA 16335
www.christianfaithpublishing.com

All scriptures are taken from the new King James version, unless specified.

Printed in the United States of America

DEDICATION

First and foremost, I dedicate this book to my Lord and savior Jesus Christ for inspiring me to write on the prayer that He himself taught His disciples to pray. I am humbled to be a vessel for such a great assignment.

To my parents: my late dad, Cleophus Nyandoro, and my mom, Agnes Mauncho Nyandoro. Thank you for your love, care, and life lessons including the prayer that you taught me.

To my children, Elizabeth and Jireh, I have learned so much by being your mother. I am grateful for the kind of responsible people you have become. I am so proud of you, and I love you.

To you, who is reading it. May you experience the treasures, the secret, and power of praying the Lord's prayer as you go through the pages of this book.

ENDORSEMENTS

"This book, "The Power of Praying the Lord's Prayer" by Sarah Nyandoro is not just a relaxing, soothing read, but it brings a new approach to prayer that I wholly endorse. Each chapter tackles a portion of the prayer in the context of the author's life. It's awfully easy to slice apart scripture and prayer with etymological scalpels, but to build a base of understanding from one's life experience is unique. Sarah has accomplished that and given the reader a blessed work that should improve their prayer life.

"I'm frequently asked to write a "blurb" or endorsement for other author's books. I almost always decline. It's hard to endorse most of them because of either subject matter or style. I had no such problem endorsing "The Power of Praying the Lord's Prayer" by Sarah Nyandoro. It is an excellent book and I wholeheartedly encourage you to purchase it and enjoy it."

Joseph Courtemanche

The Lord's Prayer is reminiscent of what a Christian should practice. This book combines a personal testimony and a teaching on prayer, based on the Lord's Prayer as taught by Jesus Christ to His disciples and recorded in Matthew 6:9-13. Sarah has put this in the perspective of the teaching by Jesus Christ as well as in the events in her personal life. This book is an encouragement to all of God's people, irrespective of denominational affiliations on how to really understand the Lord's prayer. If you believe in prayer as a way of communicating with God, this book will help you to reflect upon the Lord's Prayer in the context of your own life. With examples, it elaborates the fundamental principles and morals of Christian living drawn from the Lord's Prayer as taught by Christ Jesus. It acknowledges the supremacy of God and His authority and power, and His will for humanity, as well as His relationship with man. This book shows God's heart, His longing, and will for humanity.

Sarah has laid bare what a Christian should understand about God, whose everlasting will is to prosper man. He deserves praise, glory, and honor and He longs for a close relationship with each one of us, His people. It also elaborates on both physical and spiritual deliverances in a way that anyone can understand. I highly recommend this book to everyone in every walk of life, every age, every race, every nationality. I feel like this book can be read in every country where the Lord's prayer is taught or prayed.

Dr. B.O.N Oirere
Nairobi Kenya

When the disciples asked Jesus to "teach us how to pray" Jesus taught them the most famous and often repeated prayer the world has ever known. Each phrase reveals God's glory manifested and His grace displayed. This book shows us our Heavenly Father's daily provision from the bread of His Word and the bread of His Son, the Bread of Life. In this wilderness journey below we have not only physical but specific spiritual substance for every day. Sarah has interwoven the secret and power of praying the Lord's prayer using her own life examples that will bring a new meaning and understanding of what it means to pray the Lord's prayer to each reader. Please read this book. The revelation from God disclosed will change your life.

Pastor Judy Fornara
Spiritual Life Church
Brooklyn Center, MN.

ACKNOWLEDGMENTS

In writing this book, the following have influenced me in my life journey as well as me authoring this book.

I am grateful and indebted to my late father, Cleophus Nyandoro, and my mother, Agnes Mauncho Nyandoro, for being my first teachers of life and above all teaching me to pray, and providing an example of fervent prayer and total dependence on God. My sister, Esther Nyabonyi, you not only surrendered your clothes to me, but you taught me life lessons that I embrace even now. Thank you. Sister Margaret Nyangarisa, you are a living example of a humble and caring sister to me. You took Mom's role when I was young, as our mom was sick, going in and out of different hospitals. I am grateful to have had you in my life. To my brother, Rogers, you encouraged me in salvation as we were growing up together. Thank you bro, and keep the faith. To all my siblings, Gladys, Josephine, Dickson, Florence, Josiah, Truphen, and Grace. In one way or another, you are part of my life journey, and I want you to know that I appreciate each and every one of you. Do you remember *emiengere*? I cannot forget my later brother and late sister, Peter and Norah. You are gone before us but not forgotten. To my aunt, Milcah Oirere, and her husband, Dr. Oirere, you are a living example of a giver of both material and wisdom. Many lessons I learned from you by listening to your words of wisdom as well as watching you live by example. I am forever grateful to have had you in my life

My friends Vicky Jones (big sis as I refer to you and you call me little sis), Stella Kithinji, and Joel Reeves. You mean so much to me. Your role in my life especially in 2014 cannot be measured by words. I appreciate you.

To Mama Mercy Travis, for your steadfast assurance telling me, "Sarah, be still and know that He is God." Those words are still applicable now as they were then. Long live, Mama.

My sisters in Christ, Winnie Jason and Azie Khan, for standing with me in prayer so that God's name may be hallowed. May God bless you, and meet you at the point of your needs.

Sister Jessica, Pastor & Mrs Absalom and Esther Nasuwa, and the Umoja International Prayer Ministry for daily nourishment of the word, and the many chances you have given me to speak God's word to the prayer line. Thank you.

Thanks to my pastors, Apostle Leslie Ford and Pastor Rosella Ford, of the Living Word Church and World Outreach Ministries for your continued encouragement that God is able. Glad to have you.

To Pastors Dr. Earl F. Miller and Dr. Melvin Miller and minister Andrae Reiney, what I have learned from you through the years has made this book possible. I appreciate you. To my friend, Dr. Mary Owens, a woman of prayer that has been there for me in my trying moments, may God reward you for all you ever did and gave to me. Sisters Brenda Dean, Joanne Hill, and Victoria Stoudemire, you know your influence on me. You were God sent to rescue me. And to everyone that I may not have named, but you in one way or another influenced me, you are not forgotten. May God bless you.

Last but not least, to the most important human beings in my life, my dearly beloved children, Elizabeth and Jireh, I thank

God for giving me an opportunity to be your mother. Each one of you has taught me a life lesson that I could not have learned without you. Thank you for the life lessons God has taught me through you. May you continue to shine throughout your life journey. I love you.

Finally, to the Christian Faith Publishing team that worked on my book, for taking my manuscript and turning it into this wonderful book. You are appreciated.

FOREWORD

Sometimes when you go through tough times, you discover new ways of dealing with life issues. I am a strong believer that tough times may not seem right and fun at the moment, but it is during those tough times that we learn a lot. It is during those tough times that we grow in character. It is through trials and testing that we get upgraded. Just like in a time when we are in school or college, we get the test or exam in order to move to the next grade and next certification, so are life lessons. They come packed with challenges, trials, and huddles that we must cross. Just like when we want to build muscles, we have to strain working out, and it gets painful. But at the end, we build our strong muscles.

In life, we are in a life school every day of our lives whether we realize it or not. Each day, week, month, year, or season presents lessons to be learned. Sometimes, we learn to overcome the tests and move on, or we fail to learn and get stuck for a long time until we learn the lesson that was intended to be learned.

As for me, I can say that I learned to pray and hope in God from a very early age. I remember when I was in third grade, I had learned to read and write well, and the first thing I wanted to do was to write a letter. During those days, the only means of communicating to someone far away was through writing a letter, which you then took to a postal office to be mailed. For those who live in areas where a mailman comes to deliver your mail at the door or at your mailbox, you may not have experienced this. The post office was quite a distance.

At that young age, I wrote a letter to God, then asked my oldest sister whom I lived with to help me take the letter to the post office and mail it for me. When she asked me to whom the letter was addressed, I told her, "I have written a letter to God." She then corrected me and told me that we do not write a physical letter to mail to God, but whatever we want from God, we go to Him in prayer.

That is where my prayer life began. I won't say that every prayer was answered how I wanted it to, but I know one thing: After I prayed, I got a special kind of relief that I could not explain. Fast forward, after high school, I started reading Christian books. The funny thing I realized is that whenever I got a book to read, I looked through the table of contents; and when I saw a chapter that talks about prayer, I read that first. After reading that chapter, I felt satisfied, and sometimes I never bothered to finish reading the rest of the book. Years later, I realized that I am called to a life of prayer. I can't claim that I have been perfect in doing this, but I know that I am a work in progress. God is still working in and through me.

The Birthing of This Book

It was one of those seasons that I had sought the Lord for a breakthrough as a single mother, trying to raise my two children single-handedly that this book was birthed. I had prayed for some issues for a long time without any results and was getting anxious, not knowing what else I could do. I had prayed, confessed the word, and claimed the biblical promises, but still, no answer seemed to come my way. Instead of things getting better, they turned to get worse.

I remember this particular day back in the late summer of 2018. The situation had become too much for me to bear. I got into my car and drove to a nearby church and, just from my car, looked at the cross which is outside the entrance to that church. I had not attended that church, but all I needed was to get to see that cross. It was in the middle of the day; therefore, no one was outside or around that church compound.

Those of you who are familiar with Minnesota, know that our summers can indeed be hot and humid. At that moment, I did not know what to pray. This is because I had made my requests known to God time and time again. I asked myself, *What else am I supposed to tell God that He did not know about my situation?*

As I thought, pondered, and in what felt like a wilderness, I was tongue-tied and unable to pray, but only groaning filled with fear in my heart. Then, a phrase came to me saying, "Hallowed be thy name." This phrase repeated in my spirit as though someone was practically speaking those words to me in repeated form. This is a unique way that I have felt on a few occasions in my Christian life that I know there is something bigger than just my own thoughts. I will talk of other times that I have felt this way more in my next book, *Miracles Still Happen.* I felt in my spirit that God was telling me to humble myself and surrender the situation to Him so that in everything, His name may be hallowed. And that's exactly what I did.

In the days that followed, I contacted four sisters who were my fellow prayer warriors and told them to stand with me for the situation that was bothering me. I formed a chat group so that we could each share what the Lord was speaking to us. When they asked me what I wanted God to do in my situation, I told them that in His response, may His name be hallowed.

It is in searching this phrase in the Bible that I realized that it was taken from the Lord's Prayer. In seeking the Lord on what the phrase means and how it could apply to my situation, I started understanding that in the requests that I make, I need to ensure that God's name is glorified. That's when I started to study and search for the meaning of the whole prayer that is referred to as "The Lord's Prayer" or the "Our Father." That's when I discovered so much about the secrets and power that there is in praying this model prayer. This is how I started sectioning each section and tried to piece it together on how it can apply to our daily lives. That's when I realized that I have always recited the prayer, but now, I am discovering its power and that I can apply it to my daily life.

That is the reason I believe that the Lord gave me this title, *The Secret and Power of Praying the Lord's Prayer*, with a subtitle, *Hallowed Be Thy Name*, the phrase that I received while I was afraid and confused on what to do and what to even pray. He taught me these secrets, and now I am excited to share those secrets and the power that there is in praying the Lord's Prayer.

Therefore, I say to you, my dear reader, dive in and learn the secret and power of praying the Lord's prayer. I believe that your prayer life will never be the same.

CONTENTS

Introduction...xix

Chapter 1: Our Father, Who Art in Heaven 1
Chapter 2: Hallowed Be Thy Name................................... 12
Chapter 3: Thy Kingdom Come 24
Chapter 4: Thy Will Be Done on Earth As It Is in Heaven.... 29
Chapter 5: Give Us This Day Our Daily Bread 39
Chapter 6: And Forgive Us Our Trespasses As We
Forgive Those Who Trespass against Us 49
Chapter 7: Lead Us Not into Temptation, but
Deliver Us from Evil 56
Chapter 8: Thine Is the Kingdom, the Power, and
the Glory Forever and Ever. Amen. 62
Chapter 9: Practice Praying the Lord's Prayer 65

Conclusion.. 69

INTRODUCTION

What is prayer?

Prayer is communication with God, and it is an integral part of every Christian's life. Prayer connects us with God. There are times when one prays and, because of this, receives relief. This tends to happen more when they are in distress, when they face crossroads, or when they feel like they have reached the end of their road. It could be a one-minute utterance of a simple prayer or a groaning and crying of "oh, my God," like the servant of the man of God when he cried out to the prophet Elisha, as recorded in 2 Kings 6:15–17, "And when the servant of the man of God arose early and went out, there was an army, surrounding the city with horses and chariots. And his servant said to him, 'Alas, my master! What shall we do?' So he answered, 'Do not fear, for those who are with us are more than those who are with them.' And Elisha prayed, and said, 'LORD, I pray, open his eyes that he may see.' Then the LORD opened the eyes of the young man, and he saw. And behold, the mountain was full of horses and chariots of fire all around Elisha."

I believe most of us have been in a situation where we cried out for help from a parent, teacher, significant other, older sibling, or friend. Prayer is two-way traffic. This means that when we pray or talk to God, He will respond to us. God may speak

– xix –

through the still, small voice of the Holy Spirit, through His Word, or through other believers.

In my own life, I have had occasions when I opened the Bible and landed on a scripture that ministers to my deepest need at that moment. The first occasion I can remember of God speaking to me through His Word is when I graduated high school. For a while, I was unable to find a job or course I could join, but I finally got a part-time job away from home. Although I got this job, I had a new challenge: my employer did not pay me for over six months. As my patience was running out, I cried to God in prayer. One day, I picked up the Bible and opened the book of Revelation, and my eyes landed on verse 8 of chapter 3. It said,

> I know your works. See, I have set before
> you an open door, and no one can shut it; for
> you have a little strength, have kept My word,
> and have not denied My name. (NKJV)

At this time, I was newly saved and just beginning to trust God and wait for His help. This passage of Scripture felt like a very timely assurance that God knew my situation. I meditated on this scripture and felt that God has come to me through it to reassure me of His awareness of my situation. When I look back on my life and what I have been through, I still sense the many doors that I could not have had without God's intervention. To this day, the scripture stands true in my life. What about you? Can you recall a moment when you felt like God spoke to you through His Word?

As for God speaking to me through another person, I have an example for this as well. I had just lost my job and was going through a very difficult time in my life, and on top of this, I was a single mother with two children. When you are a single mom

Introduction

or single parent, the last thing you want to hear is that you are let go from your job. It is hard for anyone to lose a job, but it's harder when you are a single parent of two young children. It was my first time experiencing single parenting, which in itself was stressful. Now in addition, being let go from a company that I had worked for over twelve years was nerve wracking. I asked myself all the questions you can think of: how will I feed my children, how am I going to pay my rent and meet all our daily financial needs? As I will come to realize, it was one of the darkest moments of my life. (I have had my share of those dark moments in my life as I will share in my next book, in which I will show that miracles still happen.) As I drove home after my final meeting with my nurse manager and an HR representative, shocked and devastated, there was one statement I felt that God was speaking to me. It was a phrase in my mind saying, "I am not alone," and it was not once but it came repeatedly. I actually wrote it down in my journal and even shared it with one of my pastors. New challenges can bring new revelation and new solutions. I may not be able to explain it, but I felt that however lonely or alone I felt due to the surrounding circumstance, God was telling me that I was not alone. To me, that meant that he was with me and that is all that mattered.

What was even worse is that I was in the process of buying a home, only waiting for an inspection. This meant that I would be unable to proceed with the purchase of the home. To make matters worse, my lease from where I was renting at the moment had expired, and I needed proof of income in order to rent again. After I shared my situation with one of the elderly women in my church, she saw how anxious I was about what I was going through, and she stayed very calm. She said, "Sarah, be still and know that He is God."

I was scared, almost in panic mode, but this elderly woman stayed calm and kept repeating the same words: "Be still and know that God is God." And sure enough, after praying, I started feeling the calmness she showed in my own heart.

Sometimes when God speaks to us, it does not necessarily mean that things are going to change 180 degrees. Many a time, He works by changing the way we view the situations at hand, and that makes all the difference, like this situation I was in. I still was jobless. I still did not purchase the home I was in the process of buying. Being still, as the older woman kept repeating to me, helped me to calm down and was able to focus better on the next steps I had to take. Throughout my life journey, I have learned or realized that when faced with tough times or mountains, I usually pray for God to remove the mountain. His answers have been two ways. Sometimes He can move the mountain, and that is great. But other times, He does not remove the mountain, but He gives me strength to climb it.

I wonder what instances come to your mind now as you read this portion. What is that one thing that someone said to you that felt like "wow, this is it"? You may not have been in a situation exactly like mine, but someone spoke a word into your life that felt like a drop of cold water into a thirsty soul.

It is important for us to have that keen mindset of watching out to see the ways in which God may be speaking to us. Prayer changes things. We are told to pray continually. The Bible says that we need to pray without ceasing (1 Thessalonians 5:17), that by prayer and supplications, with thanksgiving, we are to make our requests known unto God.

There are so many promises in the Bible concerning prayer. We have many examples of people who prayed and received miracles, or they prayed, and the resulting changes would have not happened had they not prayed. Both the Old and the New Testament are filled with instances of God answering the prayers of His people: Hannah, mother of prophet Samuel, who was barren, and she prayed for a son, and God gave her

Introduction

Samuel; prophet Elijah at Mount Carmel with the prophets of Baal; where Elijah prayed that God may answer by fire so that it may be known that God is God. And we know that he answered by fire which consumed the sacrifice, the water, and the woods, as well as the stones, recorded in 1 Kings 18:16–38, and prophet Elisha when he asked God to open his servant's eyes to see that those who were for them were more than those who were against them.

And later, the prophet prayed to God to blind the eyes of Assyrians:

> So when *the Syrians* came down to him, Elisha prayed to the LORD, and said, "Strike these people, I pray, with blindness." And God struck them with blindness according to the word of Elisha. (2 Kings 6:8)

Their eyes were later opened at the prophet's word:

> Elisha told them, "This is not the road and this is not the city. Follow me, and I will lead you to the man you are looking for." And he led them to Samaria. After they entered the city, Elisha said, "Lord, open the eyes of these men so they can see." Then the Lord opened their eyes and they looked, and there they were, inside Samaria. (2 Kings 6:19–20)

There are many areas we can reference where people prayed both in the Bible days and even in our time. In the New Testament, we see various examples of people who came to Jesus while He was here on earth and prayed or asked Him to intervene in their situations or the situations of their loved ones or

The Secret and Power of Praying the Lord's Prayer

friend, and they were answered. An example is that of the blind Bartimaeus (Mark 10:46–52), who received his sight; Jairus's daughter, whom Jesus raised from death (Mark 5:21–43); and the crippled whom the apostles John and Peter healed in the name of Jesus (Acts 3:1–11).

When do we pray?

Many of us tend to pray more when we are facing a challenge or a difficult situation in life like sickness, tragedy, calamity, and loss. It is a last resort, not a first response. I am sure you can remember a time when you were in a terrible state because of something that had happened to you or to a loved one, those days when you knew that help would have to come from somewhere beyond you. One of those times for me was when my younger sister was battling breast cancer. I found myself praying more than I normally did. I even asked other people to come and have a prayer of agreement with me concerning her condition. If the graph could be drawn, the highest peak of our prayer life is during tragedy or difficulty.

What about you? Do you find yourself doing the same thing I did? If you do, you are not alone. But if you are one of those who are consistent in their prayer life, that is great. Some of us have yet to be there. Scripture tells us to pray without ceasing (Ephesians 6:18, 1 Thessalonians 5:17) and at the same time, pray when we are in trouble, as in Psalm 50:15: "Call upon Me in the day of trouble; I will deliver you, and you shall glorify Me."

There is also a promise given in Jeremiah 33:3 in which God promises us to show us might and greater things that we know not when we call onto Him. It is an open promise that we can be shown great and unsearchable things by God that we know not. I love that promise, for it is limitless as to what I will

Introduction

be shown. In all these, we see that we can pray at anytime and anywhere and for anything.

How should we pray?

There are many times when people utter a word of prayer in desperation, when they don't have time to do the usual procedural prayers, and they receive an answer to their prayers. Sometimes, it is even uttering the name of Jesus, and there comes an answer or solution or way out.

However, there are times when people have prayed long prayers and waited for long periods of time before they receive an answer to their prayers. There are also times when people have prayed and trusted God to move in their life situations, calling on Him, but nothing happens. In other words, or humanly speaking, their prayers are not answered.

When we have to wait for a long time or when no answer comes as we expected, it is heartbreaking. We end up asking ourselves so many *why* questions. This can be even disturbing when people around us start mocking us, saying, "How come God has not heard their cry? They have always told us to pray and that God answers prayer. Where is their answer now? Why are their children gone astray. They do drugs. They dropped out of school? Why have many other bad things happened to him/her?"

I am not saying that I have an answer to every question one might have, but I know that there are things we may not understand why they happen to us. Some things we will understand better with time, or we may never understand. Ours is to trust, obey, and surrender to Him.

In biblical times, a rabbi or teacher, taught his disciples how to pray. One example of this is John the Baptist. The Bible does not have an exact formula or pattern of the exact prayer that John taught his disciples, but we see Jesus's disciples asking Him to teach them how to pray in the first verse of chapter 11 of the Gospel of St. Luke. "Now it came to pass, as He was praying in a certain place, when He ceased, that one of His disciples (Luke 11:1) said to Him, 'Lord, teach us to pray, as John also taught his disciples.'"

Jesus's disciples had watched their Master's lifestyle and had realized that prayer was a very important part of His daily life. They had seen Him withdraw Himself from the crowd and go to a solitary place to pray; sometimes He prayed all night, as recorded in the gospel of Luke: "Now it came to pass in those days that He went out to the mountain to pray, and continued all night in prayer to God" (Luke 6:12). Other times, they had watched Him wake up early before dawn and leave to go to a solitary place to spend time in prayer. Another example is in the Gospel according to Mark: "Very early in the morning, while it was still dark, Jesus got up, left the house and went off to a solitary place, where he prayed" (Mark 1:35).

We need to understand that rabbis often composed prayers for their disciples to recite. When Jesus's disciples watched Him pray, they must have come to realize that this wasn't just a recital prayer. They admired His prayer life and, therefore, asked Him to teach them to pray. Before this, they had watched Him do miracles, heal the sick, cast out demons, and do countless other miracles. It seems that the disciples, having seen the impact of Jesus's prayer on His teachings and miracles, were moved to ask for the source of the power, which they had realized to be His prayer life. They asked to know how to pray, which is the source of all power to do all miracles. They knew that prayer would connect them to the source, God the Father.

Their request to their Master to be taught prayer, which is the backbone of all power, reminds me of the prayer that was offered by a young king, Solomon. He did not ask for riches,

Introduction

treasure, or fame, but he asked God to give him wisdom on how to rule over His people.

> That night God appeared to Solomon and asked, "What would you like me to give you?" Solomon answered, "You always showed great love for my father David, and now you have let me succeed him as king. O Lord God, fulfill the promise you made to my father. You have made me king over a people who are so many that they cannot be counted, so give me the wisdom and knowledge I need to rule over them. Otherwise, how would I ever be able to rule these great people of yours?" (1 Chronicles 1:7–9)

Just as King Solomon knew that success in his role as king would be brought about by wisdom that only God could give, so the disciples knew that their success in following and doing the will of God would be through learning from their Master how to pray.

Like King Solomon and the Lord's disciples, we too need to understand the power of prayer. Prayer will cause real change, will draw us closer to God, and will give us peace that surpasses all human understanding. I would like to remind us that we don't necessarily pray to change God, but praying helps us to be in tune with God's purpose for our lives. So as the disciples asked their Master to teach them to pray, let us also ask the Lord to teach us to pray using the model prayer that He taught His disciples that has come to be known as the Lord's Prayer or the Abba Father.

The Lord's Prayer

The Lord's Prayer has been with us from the time of Jesus's ministry here on earth. It is a common prayer that is recited in many Christian denominations. The Catholic Church recites it in almost every mass, and many of the congregants have memorized the Lord's Prayer. Both my parents were and still are Catholics. Therefore, it is from them that I first learned how to recite the Lord's Prayer. Being Catholics, Mom and Dad taught us (my siblings and I) to recite several different prayers, and one of the ones we learned early in life was the Lord's Prayer. This was reinforced more as I moved to live with my older sister and joined a Catholic-sponsored primary school. We students knew how to recite both the Rosary and the Lord's Prayer by heart.

Even though I learned the Lord's Prayer at an early age, I did not understand what it meant. It did feel good to pray it daily, but I did not give it much thought, nor do I remember being taught in-depth how to use it, outside of reciting it. I believe that I am not alone. Maybe, as you are reading this book, you discover that you, too, have never given it deep thought and have never been taught how to pray the Lord's Prayer outside of memorization and recitation.

But if you have had the opportunity to be taught or to teach the details of the Lord's Prayer, I ask that you give me a chance to bring the importance of this powerful prayer to you. I know that there is power even in reciting it as most of us have done for most of our lives. A friend of mine told me that for her, when she is having a difficult time, she recites the Lord's Prayer ten times; by the time she is done, she has the strength to go through whatever she is struggling with. I know that there is power in repetition, and as she repeats it aloud, those words become imprinted in her mind. And as she hears herself speaking the words of the prayer repeatedly, faith rises, for the word

Introduction

says in the book of Romans that faith "comes by hearing and hearing by the word of God" (Romans 10:17).

Now let us dive into this together and see what the Lord has for us. Let us see what was in His heart when He taught them this amazing prayer that is referred to as the Lord's Prayer. Walk with me as I, by the help of the Holy Spirit, bring out the riches and wonders that are hidden in this powerful prayer, the Lord's Prayer.

Father in Jesus's name, I pray Thee that as I expound on what You have been teaching me about the prayer that our Lord Jesus taught His disciples to pray, may the Holy Spirit minister to me first then through me so that as I put His riches into words, whoever reads this book or hears about the contents of this book may be drawn closer to You, that everyone, including myself, will experience the power that there is in praying this powerful prayer, that You will reveal what was in Your heart, Lord Jesus, when You taught Your disciples to pray in this manner.

It is my prayer, dear Lord Jesus, that You use me, Your handmaiden, as a vessel. Only You speak through me, for without You, I can do nothing. It is Your model prayer that You taught Your disciples to pray. Therefore, Lord, teach us to pray. I ask all these in Jesus's name. Amen.

The Lord's Prayer is not only recited in the Catholic Church but other Christian denominations as well. I attended Seventh-day Adventist churches for two years, and I realized that they, too, have a time during the service when they kneel and pray the Lord's Prayer. In many Pentecostal churches, there are times at the end of prayer or petitioning when the leader says, "Now let us pray the prayer that Jesus taught his disciples to pray." Then the congregation recites the Lord's Prayer.

– xxix –

Those of us who grew up going to church or who had churchgoing family members have heard the Lord's Prayer, and most can recite it. I wonder if you have ever had a chance to really think about what it means. What was in the mind of the Lord Jesus Christ when He chose this specific formula, telling His disciples that when they pray, they should pray in that manner?

In the pages of this book, I will dive into the Lord's Prayer and, by the grace of God and through the leading of the Holy Spirit, I will elaborate on what it really means. We will see that it was not meant to be simply recited and left at that. We will see that it can be a way of enriching our daily lives and that it encompasses any area of our lives for which we could ever think to pray, such as adoration, worship, interceding for others, relationships with our fellow men, and our walk with God. We will see that it was meant to be a guide, not just a recitation. My prayer is that, by reading this book, you will be able to understand the prayer, and you will be able to enrich your prayer life by understanding and practicing it, that you will draw near to God as He longs to draw near to you. It does not matter if you are already familiar with the Lord's Prayer or if it is your first time hearing and reading about it. I pray that you will read this prayer with a prayerful heart and see God enriching and transforming your daily prayer life through it. Let us begin.

Let us look at the model prayer that is referred to as the Lord's Prayer. We will first read it out aloud as it is written in the Gospel according to Matthew. I will ask that we read it slowly and thoughtfully. Here it is:

> Our Father, who art in heaven, hallowed
> be thy name, thy kingdom come, thy will
> be done on earth as it is in heaven. Give us
> this day, our daily bread and forgive us our

Introduction

trespasses, as we forgive those who trespass against us. Lead us not into temptation, but deliver us from evil. For thine is the kingdom, the power and the glory both now and forever more. Amen. (Matthew 6:9–13)

I was a schoolteacher back in Kenya, where I was born and raised, before I moved to the US. I have lived here in the United States for over twenty-two years. For those of you who are teachers, you know that a teacher makes a scheme of work at the start of the semester. That is how education was organized in Kenya while I was there, and I think this still continues. The scheme of work is a summary, like a series of headlines, of the work that is expected to be covered for a period of time called a term or semester. The teacher uses this scheme of work as a guideline to teach students in that particular class or subject.

The schemes of work were derived from the syllabus according to the requirements of the ministry of education of that particular grade. The teacher derives daily lessons geared toward meeting the objectives of that day in alignment with the schemes of work that he or she had already prepared. In my experience, the lesson plan for each day went into depth explaining the specific subject matter in detail so that the students would be able to understand it.

Often, at the end of the lesson, the teacher may give some exercises to the students to reinforce their understanding of the subject matter. If I teach my students to memorize my scheme of work, they will memorize it, but they will miss the whole point of the subject matter. The scheme of work is a guideline, but the daily lesson plan brings out the rich content and application of what is being taught/learned. Therefore, a good teacher will not only teach their students to memorize the les-

– xxxi –

son but will strive to ensure that the students understand and can apply what they learned by answering test questions.

The Lord Jesus, Himself the teacher or rabbi of His disciples, would have meant for the prayer He taught them to be more than just a recitation. It was meant to guide them in areas about which they needed to pray, areas that were important for them to remember as they approached God in prayer. I see Christ's prayer as a scheme of work, almost like a human teacher's scheme of work. Christ, being the Son of God and the Son of Man who came from the Father, knows what touches the heart of God when people pray. Therefore, He gave His disciples a scheme of work that they needed to develop and put into practice.

When we recite the Lord's Prayer, we are like students memorizing their teacher's scheme of work. Another way to put it is this: I see it as a skeleton. As we all know, the skeleton is very important for the form of the body. However, the skeleton still needs tendons, ligaments, flesh, and skin to make the body functional and complete.

Now, in the pages that follow, I, with the help of the Holy Spirit, will do my absolute best to unpack the Lord's Prayer in order to bring it to our daily lives. I will also try to point out from Scripture where the Lord Jesus applied the model prayer in His own prayer, His life, His teachings, and the miracles that He performed as recorded in the Holy Scripture.

Walk with me as we learn to apply the Lord's Prayer to our daily prayer lives. My prayer for each and every one who will read this book is that faith will arise in you, that you will experience the power that there is in praying the Lord's Prayer, and that you will have a taste of what the Teacher had in mind when He uttered the words of this prayer in response to the request put forth unto Him by His disciples, saying, "Lord, teach us to

Introduction

pray, even as John taught his disciples to pray." When you pray, pray in this manner.

Our Father, who art in heaven, hallowed be thy name, thy kingdom come, thy will be done on earth as it is in heaven. Give us this day, our daily bread and forgive us our trespasses, as we forgive those who trespass against us. Lead us not into temptation, but deliver us from evil. For thine is the kingdom, the power, and the glory, both now and forevermore. Amen.

CHAPTER 1

Our Father, Who Art in Heaven

There are several areas in the Old Testament where people prayed to God. The first person we see praying to God is Abraham when he pleaded with God on behalf of Sodom and Gomorrah when he got word that the two cities were going to be destroyed by fire from heaven, as recorded in Genesis 18:16–33. King David also prayed to God the Father in 1 Chronicles 20:10. We also see King Solomon praying at the dedication of the Jerusalem temple.

I think it will be beneficial to first look at who Jesus is before we discuss the prayer He taught His disciples. Jesus is both man and God. John starts his gospel by calling Jesus the Word that became flesh and dwelt among us, and John continues by saying that Jesus was in the beginning with God and was God. The name that was revealed to Joseph by the angel of the Lord before Christ was born was Immanuel, which means "God with us."

Jesus the Son of God and the Son of Man came to unite humanity with their Creator, God. As He taught them the Lord's Prayer, His main goal was to show, through His teaching and lifestyle, that God had come to be with His people, which was the meaning of His name, Immanuel. As we dive into this

The Secret and Power of Praying the Lord's Prayer

rich prayer that Jesus taught His disciples, we shall do it knowing the background of the one who taught it, the Lord Jesus Christ, and see Him bringing God and His people together.

The Lord's Prayer starts with a relationship phrase. It shows the connection between the one who is praying and the object of the prayer. The prayer begins with "Our Father, who art in heaven." The recording of the Lord's Prayer is the first time that we see Jesus teaching His disciples about relationships. Jesus often used examples in His teaching that the people He taught could relate to. He quite often used day-to-day examples to express the points He taught, like the Prodigal Son, the Lost Sheep, the Sower, and the Soils. As we read this first section, we see that a father is a common image to most people. Now let us look at the following: What does a father do, and what does he expect of his children?

What does a father do? A father is the head of the household. He provides, protects, teaches, leads, corrects, and challenges us to do better; he not only thinks of today but also plans for our tomorrow; he not only spends money on food and on bills, but he puts something aside for vacation, for a rainy day, as well as for college. Perhaps you are reading this and saying, "I never had a father," or "My father never did this for us, only mom did, for he was hardly ever there." Whatever it was like when you were growing up or whatever situation you were in or are in at this moment, know that I hear you. If your mom, an uncle or an aunt, or someone else fulfilled the role of a father, I hope that you can use this image instead of the image of a father.

What does a father expect from his children? He expects trust and obedience, which will remove fear from them. He expects his children to ask for help and to believe him. In other words, there is a special relationship between a father and his children. It is the father's pleasure to be there for his kids in good and bad times. But things can be different when one of the parties does not fulfill their role, whether it be the father not providing for his children or the children disobeying their father. Take a few moments and reflect on the role your father (or a father figure if you did not have a father in your life) played in your life even until now.

From the very beginning, Jesus's name, Immanuel, means, "God is with us." He came to connect us to God the Father. Teaching them to approach God as their Father, He wanted His disciples to know that He not only connected them in a casual way but that He shares His Father with them. God the Father is their Father as well. As it is written in the Gospel according to John,

> But as many as received Him, to them He gave the right to become children of God, to those who believe in His name, who were born not of blood, nor of the will of the flesh, nor of the will of man, but of God. (John 1:12–13)

Even you and I, as long as we have fulfilled the above scripture, are God's children. Believe it and approach Him as so.

Jesus had to tell them who they were to God and who He was to them. The father-child relationship is very close. He wanted them to know that God is their Father and that as their father He already knows them. There is a special sense of assurance when you talk to your own father that you do not get when you talk to a stranger or even to your boss or friends. We see this mostly in little children. They can run and tell their dad anything, but they cannot even talk if it is a stranger.

In our natural life, the father is the head of the home. The father provides leadership in the home. He provides counseling.

He is the one who protects the family in the event of an attack from enemies. The father works and earns money so the family can buy necessities and pay bills. In the old days, the dad worked outside of the home, and the mom worked in the home. There is such a great trust that children place in their fathers, such that if anyone is messing with one of them, they say, "You just wait until my *dad* comes!" The children believe that their dad is the most powerful force on planet earth. I know most of us can remember a time when we either could not do something or were afraid, but Dad showed up, and we felt a sense of calm and relief.

Under normal circumstances, the joy of every father is to be there for his family. It gives him pride that his children trust him for everything. I say "under normal circumstances" because there are obviously some cases of fathers taking the lives of their children or molesting them. There are some other unfortunate cases where a father may be deceased, imprisoned, or he is physically or mentally incapacitated, which makes it impossible for him to provide the fatherly role as he should and as he could have loved to. There are even more cases where children do not know who their father is, or he is absent from their lives. Reportedly, the mother is most often the parent who remains in single-parent households. If you happen to be one of the children who have experienced this, know that you are not alone. These are special cases where children will not experience the relationship of a father with his children. And that's the reason I say "under normal circumstances."

The other aspect we see in this approach of "our Father" is that the father has the final say; the children know what they want, but the father knows what the children need. In addressing God as Father, we give Him room to say, "Yes," "No," or "Wait." The disciples learned, when they first approached the Father, that there are some requests God grants immediately

Our Father, Who Art in Heaven

and some which the disciples will have to wait to receive; there are also some that they may never get. That is what a father does. This shows that the father is in control and the giver of all good things.

We see many instances in the Bible where people prayed and had to wait for a long time for their requests to be answered, and we also see many whose prayers were never answered as expected. Some of those who had to wait for a long time are Hannah, the mother of the prophet Samuel (1 Samuel 1:1–28, 2:1–11); Zacharias and Elizabeth, the parents of John the Baptist (Luke 1:5–25); and the parents of Samson (Judges 13:1–24). Not only did they wait patiently for a long period of time, but they were given an answer to their prayers that could not have come earlier.

It was God-ordained that the prayers be granted at the right time on God's calendar, not theirs. It happened that, as the parents were waiting patiently to have children, God's plan was to give them a child who fulfilled their purpose and God's purpose. Take the example of Elizabeth and Zachariah. They waited until old age, but God planned for them to have their child close to the time when Jesus was born because he was a forerunner of Jesus.

What about Hannah, mother to the prophet Samuel? God waited to not only give Hannah a son but also a prophet for His people Israel. As Hannah was pregnant with her son, Samuel, Israel was pregnant with her prophet, who was their first one after Moses. This shows us that God's purpose is bigger than man's purpose. God does not always tell us why things happen the way they do. In His mind and plan, He had chosen Hannah to be the mother of one of the greatest men in Bible history. The tough thing for Hanna was that she had no idea what God's plan for her womb was. Although she was bitter because of the way her co-wife mocked her, she knew that her answer lied in

God's hands. That is why she poured her heart to God asking for a son. I want you to stop and look at your prayers, and the "no" answer seems to come. You feel like God is not hearing you, and you are almost giving up. The enemy of your soul is telling you, "If God is on your side, where is He now?" Could it be that many of the prayers you think are unanswered have nothing to do with you, but God is delaying them purposefully in order to fulfill something bigger? Keep on trusting and keep on believing. His plans for you are for good and not for evil, to give you a future and to give you hope. So I say wait on the Lord. May He renew your strength as you wait on Him. He is faithful, and in time, He will surely come through for you.

Something that is common to those parents whom I have mentioned is that they did not drift away from serving God because their prayers seemed to be unanswered. They continued steadfastly serving and fulfilling their responsibilities as they prayed for their miracles. What do we do when we wait for a week, a month, a year, or longer and no sign of an answer to our prayer comes? Do we keep on trusting and believing, or do we get frustrated and give up? What do we do when people ridicule us, saying, "Where is the God she talks about? Where is the power of prayer she talks about?" What do we do when our version of Hannah's Peninnah mocks us? I pray that we keep on believing even when we don't see why, for God knows, and He is always on time. When we pray, the answer can be "yes," "wait," or "no." He knows. He is the Father.

With this understanding, the disciples would not be disappointed when they received any of the three answers to their prayers. Jesus did not want to raise entitled disciples who thought that approaching God would be like going through a drive-through and asking for your order. He wanted them to acknowledge Him as their Father.

Our Father, Who Art in Heaven

I can say that if they needed to know that then, we in our day need to know it more in our twenty-first century. This is because we live in a drive-through, fast-Internet computer culture. We are used to going to Google and getting our questions answered in an instant. We have fast food that is quick to get. We have microwaves that make cooking or warming our foods easy. A friend is a phone call, a text, or an email away.

Our generation will have to be intentional if they want to practice waiting. Waiting is the hardest thing to do in our time. The nature of our lives wants things in an instant, or else we get bored waiting. Check on both adults and younger people and see how many times you hear/see boredom. "I am bored," says most of our younger generation. I don't know about you, but even in my own life, waiting creates anxiety. Our Lord Jesus, who is all knowing, sees our generation's desire to know things quickly. He taught us to address the Father and to make room in our hearts to be content, whether He grants our request there and then or has us wait for the right time or even when He says no.

Although some may not have had fathers in the home at all, God can be everyone's Father. As you address Him as "our Father," allow Him to do what a good father does for his children. If your father was not present in the home as you grew up, allow God to be the Father. He says in His Word that He is the Father to the fatherless and a defender of the widowed (Psalms 68:5). No matter what has happened, ask Him to help you see His love for you. If you were abused or abandoned by your earthly father, you can safely let God into your life. Even if you did not have a good experience of what a father truly is, you can allow God to be your true Father. Bear this in mind as you enter into this powerful prayer that is going to revolutionize your prayer life and empower you as you have never seen.

The Secret and Power of Praying the Lord's Prayer

We all know that we don't live in a perfect world. As we cover this first portion of the Lord's Prayer, I would like you to pause and ask yourself this question: do you see yourself in light of being a child of God, according to John 1:12 (NIV), which says, "But to all who did receive him, who believed in his name, He gave the right to become children of God"? If your answer is yes, praise God for that! If it is no or if you are not sure, consider believing in Him and by faith become His child. The Bible says, "If you confess with your mouth the Lord Jesus and believe in your heart that God raised Him from the dead, you will be saved" (Romans 10:9). This helps us as we proceed in the Lord's Prayer, that we are assured of approaching Him as Father and us His children.

What are some of the prayers you have prayed and haven't seen answered? What are some of the prayers you have prayed where the answer was not what you expected? Maybe you prayed for healing for a sick loved one, but they died instead. Maybe a tragedy happened that changed your life forever. It is not easy to go through that. I had a sister who was battling breast cancer over ten years ago. I prayed and sought help from other believers for her healing. She lost the battle and went home to be with the Lord. She left five young children ranging from the ages of five to thirteen. I don't know why, and I don't have an answer as to why my prayers and the prayers of many for her healing did not yield the expected results. Some things we as human beings may not understand in this life, but we are told to trust and obey.

The same thing happened a year later when my eldest brother died of a stroke. However, these and many other unanswered prayers do not mean that I don't have prayers that have been answered. I have seen great breakthroughs in my Christian walk, and I can look back and see God's mighty hand at work.

I have learned to trust in Him and to depend upon His Word. His joy has been my strength.

Our earthly fathers can say "yes," "no," or "wait" in answer to our requests. But at the same time, our heavenly Father does more than what His children ask. He anticipates and even provides the child with what is necessary even if the child has not asked. One example we can see is the one in the parable of the Prodigal Son in Luke 15:11–32, the son said to himself when he came to his senses that he would go back home and ask his father not to call him a son but to take him in as a servant. But the father did the opposite. He got the servants to give him nice clothes and slaughtered the fattest calf, and there was a great celebration.

God does that for us. He accepts us just the way we are. He is waiting for us to come to our senses and return to Him. He will wash us from all unrighteousness with the blood of Jesus, which means the forgiveness of our sins, then the angels in heaven will have a big party. Jesus tells us that "there is great rejoicing in the presence of the angels of God over one sinner who repents" (Luke 15:10). Sometimes we mess up big-time and feel like we are not worthy to return to him. Remember, He tells us to come to Him just as we are. Isaiah 1:18 says the following: "'Come now, and let us reason together,' says the LORD, 'Though your sins are like scarlet, They shall be as white as snow; Though they are red like crimson, They shall be as wool.'" Also in 1 John 1:9, the Bible says the following: "If we confess our sins, He is faithful and just to forgive us *our* sins and to cleanse us from all unrighteousness." This means that no matter what sins you think you have done, He is able and willing to forgive you. He is a good father.

The Father sometimes goes the extra mile to give us what we have not asked for because He knows what we need before we even ask Him. Sometimes He sees our helplessness and just does what an earthly father would do. Consider Jairus's daughter in the fifth chapter of the book of Mark. She did not ask her dad to go find a cure, but her dad did what needed to be done. Whenever a situation arises, dad gets into action to do what a dad does. He went and begged Jesus to come heal his daughter.

Also, in the story of the boy who was possessed by a demon as recorded in Mark 9:14–24, his father said, "I believe, help my unbelief." He was pleading for his son. God is our Father; He will do more for us than our earthly fathers will ever be able to do. Jesus said to His disciples, "If you then, being evil, know how to give good gifts to your children, how much more will your Father who is in heaven give good things to those who ask Him!" (Matthew 11:7).

Let us continue and say the sample prayer for this section:

Father, in the name of Your Son Jesus Christ, thank You for being my Father, as Your Word says. Help me to approach You as Father, knowing that You have my best interests at heart. I thank You, for You love me as Your child, and You are able. As a father loves his children and provides for them, I thank You that You are even more able than that because You are the Creator of the universe.

Sometimes I have asked for things which I have received, and for that, I thank You. There are others that I have asked You for and have not seen any sign of the answers yet. Help me to not give up. Help me, Father, to continue trusting in You and waiting on You.

There are prayers I have prayed, and the answer did not come; as a human being, I felt that my prayers were not answered. Help me, Father, not to be disheartened by the unanswered prayers. Knowing that You will cause all things to work for my good, I believe and trust in You. Help me, dear Lord, to know that even when I don't see You, or when I don't hear You, or when I don't feel You, You are still there and that You are causing all things to work for my good because I love and trust in You as Your Word tells me in Romans 8:28. Thank You, Father, for being my Father. In Jesus's name I pray. Amen.

Let us trust God as our Father and know that while sometimes we may not understand right away, we will understand better by and by. Take a moment and pray in your own words to God as Father. Tell Him what you feel in your heart and ask Him to help you as a father helps his child.

CHAPTER 2

Hallowed Be Thy Name

The second part of the Lord's Prayer is the sentence "hallowed be thy name." According to the English dictionary, *to hallow* is *to make or set apart as holy, to respect or honor greatly, or to revere.* We hallow only those whom we treat with awe and respect, those who deserve it.

In this section of the prayer, we ask God that in all we do, in all we say, or in all we think about, we may revere or hallow His name, that our lives—by word, thought, and deed—may reflect the glory and honor of His name. This section calls for us to be intentional in what we say, what we do, and what we think about to ensure that we reflect and glorify God: *hallowed be the name of the Lord.*

I would like you to pause for a moment here and reflect on what you have spoken, what you have done, and what you have been thinking since the day began. Was it glorifying God? Sometimes we say things and call it a slip of the tongue. Sometimes we are so used to a certain way of speaking that we are now realizing that it doesn't glorify God. If it has been a habit, it might take time to change it, but it is doable. It is time to examine yourself in light of the Word of God. Ask Him to

Hallowed Be Thy Name

help you overcome some of the habits that do not give glory to His name.

The apostle Paul's letter to the church at Philippi says the following:

> Finally, brethren, whatever things are true, whatever things are noble, whatever things are just, whatever things are pure, whatever things are lovely, whatever things are of good report, if there is any virtue and if there is anything praiseworthy—meditate on these things. (Philippians 4:8)

We can practice this in our daily lives, intentionally choosing what we focus our thoughts on. It does not come easy, but with practice and prayer, we can learn to redirect our thoughts so that God is hallowed in them. Just as the psalmist says, "Let the words of my mouth and the meditations of my heart be acceptable in Your sight, O Lord, my strength and my Redeemer" (Psalm 19:14). Consciously ensuring that what we speak and think about may glorify the name of the Lord our God is one of the ways that God's name may be hallowed in our lives. This is because all actions start with a thought. Therefore, guard your mind so that you may glorify God in all you do.

What is in a name?

A name identifies a person. A name comes with power and with authority. Remember when you were young, those times when your sibling told you to do something. At times you refused, but if they said, "Dad said," you had to think twice about your refusal, whether the authority was a parent, a teacher, or a school principal. A name is important. Or at your place of work, the manager or director of an organization has the power to hire and fire. Many times, when we read an e-mail from an authority, we better take notice of any warning we may come across or any new inventions they are implementing in the workplace. The man or woman with a name or title with authority has power.

There are many examples in our daily lives of a leader displaying the power in their name. Be it a governor ordering the mandatory wearing of masks due to a pandemic or a president signing an executive order or bill, it is because of the power of that name or title. Some people have been hired in a position because of who they know. And sometimes people have received better services than they could have received because they knew or were sent there by an authority figure. This happened more when I was in Kenya.

What is in the name of God?

The author of Proverbs says the following: "the name of the Lord is a strong tower, the righteous run into it and they are safe" (Proverbs 18:10). There is safety in the name of the Lord. Let His name be hallowed and you will find safety when you run unto it. Safety is provided and is assured. It is our responsibility to make the choice to run unto it, and when we do, we will find safety. In God's name, there is salvation, as it is written in the book of Romans, "Everyone who calls on the name of the Lord will be saved" (Romans 10:13). Make a decision to call on His name and you will find salvation.

In His name, there is freedom. His name *is Jehovah Jireh, the Lord who provides* (Genesis 22:14). He will provide all that we need. In His name, there is peace because He is *Jehovah Shalom, the Lord of peace* (Judges 6:24). There are several instances in the Bible where the Bible states what we can get when we pray in the name of Jesus. He gave His disciples many promises that they will have when they use His name; examples are in John 15:7, where He told them that if they abide in Him and His Word abides in them, then they can ask for anything, and it shall be given them.

Also in the same book, chapter 16, verse 24, where Jesus tells them this: "until now, you have asked nothing in my name, ask, and you will receive, that your joy may be full." There is power in the name of Jesus. It is the name we were given to use against the powers of the enemy of our souls.

We are daily surrounded by situations and issues in life that leave us without peace. They leave us anxious, on edge, depressed, and sometimes hopeless. We even sometimes lack peace. Well, He is our peace. The New Testament talks about what the Lord will do for us when we pray.

> Do not be anxious about anything, but in everything, by prayer and supplication with thanksgiving make your requests known unto God, and the peace of God which transcends all understanding, will guard your hearts and minds through Christ Jesus. (Philippians 4:6–7)

This means that anxiety is all around us, that we can sometimes get carried away by anxiety, and that anxiety targets our hearts and our minds. It doesn't matter how much wealth we have, how famous we are, how rich we are; if our minds are attacked, fame and wealth suddenly mean very little. It is the peace of mind that matters most.

If you look deep into your own life, there must be times when things were not going well for you. Maybe you were dealing with abuse of some kind. Maybe you were dealing with rejection. Maybe you were dealing with sickness in you or in a family member. Maybe you were dealing with the fear, the anxiety, and the "what ifs" in the night. Your beauty, wealth, or fame didn't matter; what mattered was the situation at hand.

Paul is telling us that after we fulfill verse 6 of chapter 4 of Philippians, then the peace of God, which surpasses all our understanding, will guard our hearts and minds in Christ Jesus. It is the peace that God gives us that guards and protects our hearts and minds in Christ Jesus, not our money, fame, education, beauty, or even what other people think of us but the peace of God. If it were riches, good houses, expensive vehicles or materials that gave peace, then the rich would not be stressed, or they would not lack peace at all. But it is only the peace of God that guards our heart and minds in Christ Jesus.

There was a time at the beginning of 2018 when I found myself very anxious about a situation that was going on in my family. I had reached the point where I was unable to get a good night's sleep. I would go to bed, and it would take a long time to fall asleep. I was not only taking a long time to fall asleep, but I could not stay asleep. Some nights, I would wake up after only two hours at about 1:00 a.m. and am unable to sleep until 4:00 a.m., just tossing and turning. I was getting exhausted at work early on in the day.

One morning, I read Philippians 4:6–7, and it struck me in a new way. I wrote it down and personalized it. This is how I made it to minister to me: First, at the top of a piece of paper, I copied out the verses. Next, I rewrote it this way:

Father, I am not going to be anxious about a, b, c, and here I inserted my fears: eg about my diagnosis, my relationships, my children's education, their friendships, their health, and many other issues. But, by prayer and supplications with thanksgiving, I make these requests known unto you. (I named those things that were

stressing me up) And your peace which transcends all my under-
standing will keep my heart and mind through Christ Jesus.

I placed that paper on my nightstand. I read it aloud at least twice every day. I realized that it is after I fulfilled verse 6 that the fulfillment of verse 7 will come to pass.

Every time the anxiety started to kick in and I found myself worrying, I read that scripture with the personalized version of it. The more I read this and confessed it aloud, the less intense the anxiety and worry became. By the end of one week of repeating this consistently, my fears and anxiety were much less intense, and I found the peace of God; after some time, I again rewrote verse 7 and confessed it this way. The peace of God that I have keep my heart and mind in Christ Jesus. I realized that by so saying, I am claiming that peace, that I have it already and that my heart is being kept in Christ Jesus. This has been coming handy for me time and time again. I just repeat it when I am faced with some overwhelming situations, and it does help.

I am sure it won't take everyone exactly a week to get better from those issues that are making you anxious, but I suggest that you try this: hallow the name of God, our peace. Make sure to read it aloud. I have realized that there is a difference when I read something out loud. By reading aloud, I am engaging the sense of hearing, remembering that in the book of Romans, the Bible says the following: "Faith comes by hearing, and hearing by the word of God" (Romans 10:17). Therefore, as I engage the sense of hearing, I am building my faith. I used to think that this verse only meant that I have to have someone preach the word to me. I came to realize that I can hear the Word when I read it aloud. There is something about hearing, and I now try to read the word aloud whenever circumstances allow. I have seen a significant difference.

Try it and see for yourself; pick some of the promises of God and speak them to yourself aloud. Take the example of the verse in Psalm 139, which talks about how fearfully and wonderfully you were made. This is not being proud, but it is calling yourself the same thing that God calls you. You may or may know someone close who struggles with self-acceptance. This may be because we go by what other people have called us repeatedly, and it has built into our own self. We have believed that we are not cute enough, not skinny enough, not tall enough, not educated enough, not talented enough, and the list goes on. I will say this to you who find yourself in any of the above or even what I have not mentioned, do yourself a favor, say the above verse, and repeat it every morning and when you go to bed. Write down what you feel after three, seven, fourteen days of repetition. It may not change your features, but it will change how you look at yourself.

Also, jot down those issues that seem to worry you most of the time. Personalize the verses above, like I did. With prayer, you will start to see a difference. It may not happen the first or second or even third time. The point is to keep repeating the Word as often as the fear comes; you meet the fear with the Word of God. Why would you be tired of saying what the Word says when the fear and anxiety has not slowed down or gotten tired of bothering you? This is not a one-time fix. It is a continued battle, but know that you are a winner because the God who has promised is faithful and will fulfill His Word for the glory and honor of His name. Hebrews 10:23 says the following: "Let us hold fast to the confession of our faith without wavering, for He who promised is faithful." The "promiser" is faithful. What will help us to receive the promise is our unwavering confession of our faith in His promises. Think about this for a moment and let it sink in. Do you see how important your speech is? Check and evaluate what you have been confess-

Hallowed Be Thy Name

ing. Correct whatever is not in alignment with God's promises. Replace and start confessing what His word says. I have given an example above. Note what happens when you change your speech; faith will rise in you.

The name of God is to be hallowed. It is to be greatly respected and revered. When the Lord Jesus taught His disciples this part of prayer, I believe that He was telling them the kind of a name the name of God is. Think about the conversations you have on a daily basis with your family members, coworkers, and strangers. The question that each one of us should ask ourselves is this: who is being hollowed in what I am saying, thinking, or doing? We could be doing a charitable act, but at the back of our minds, we could be looking for recognition and praise. The Father's name should be glorified in all we do. When you preach, ask yourself, who is being glorified? Do you find yourself saying, "I am the best! Nobody can preach like me"? It takes humility to surrender, and surrendering to God is called for in this section so that only His name is hallowed or glorified.

In all our prayers, we must ask, "Who will be honored when I accomplish this or that?" The bottom line must be that we want the name of the Lord to be honored. This section of the Lord's Prayer is telling us that honoring the Lord doesn't come automatically, that it takes a conscious decision as to who is going to be honored. Jesus told His disciples that the name of the Father is to be honored. That is the foundation of the whole picture, that whatever we are praying for, whatever miracle we are asking God to do, His name will be honored above all. That means that when our prayers are answered, His name will be honored; it is all about Him.

I was recently faced with a challenging situation that made me restless. I found myself pacing the halls at work; I did not know what to do. It was psychologically intense. You know those things that happen, and it is suddenly like you are left

– 19 –

at sea, like you don't know what it is that hit you. You wish to know what it is so you can see how to fix it. You realize that there is a problem, but you have no way of knowing what it is.

A good example for those who are in the United States is this: you learn that the person you love is in the hospital. You want to call and find out, but the nurses tell you, "We have no release of information. Therefore, we can't even tell you whether the person is here, let alone tell you what the problem is." For those in my homeland country and similar places, I want to give you a warning: there is what they call the Health Insurance Portability and Accountability Act (HIPAA) privacy. In order for a family member or friend to talk to hospital staff about their loved one in the hospital or clinic, there has to be a signed release of information by the patient to allow that to happen. Without it, they will not release any information about the patient, including acknowledgement that he or she is in that facility. If they do, they have violated the HIPAA privacy and may undergo disciplinary actions.

When you are at the receiving end, it is not fun. I have been at both ends, and I know how each one feels. But as I prayed this part of the Lord's Prayer, I zeroed in on it and prayed, "Father, when this gets solved, Your name will be hallowed. When people hear of it, Your name will be hallowed. When this child succeeds/healed, Your name will be hallowed. I have trusted in You, and I am called by Your name.

"If this turns out bad and the child does not succeed or they go astray, Your name will not be hallowed. People will start saying, 'She claimed that God is with her and that He would never leave her nor forsake her, and they might start mocking Your name. So, Father, may Your name be hallowed. You have said in Psalm 84:11 that no good thing would You withhold from those who love You. I surrender this to You that at the end of it all, Your name will be hallowed."

Hallowed Be Thy Name

I had the peace of God. I started talking to three sisters who joined me in praying for this situation. After explaining to them what was going on, they asked me what I wanted them to ask God to do. I found myself giving them this phrase: "That His name may be hallowed in it." We have prayed, and although at this time I have not seen tangible evidence, I believe that the name of the Lord is hallowed in it. All is working for my good, for I trust in Him for His glory.

I would like you to look back into those prayers that you have been presenting before the Lord. Reflect on what we have discussed so far. Have you been praying according to the Lord's Prayer, according to the way we have discussed in this section? Is what you have prayed for going to hallow the name of the Lord? It may not be easy to transition immediately into praying this kind of prayer, but God will help you.

Although He is willing to help you, you have to purpose to come to Him positively so that you want His name to be hallowed in your life. Also, at the end of each prayer request, ask Him to show you where you have not fully allowed room for His name to be hallowed. Allow His name to be hallowed in your life: in the way you talk, *in the way you dress*, and in your verbal and nonverbal expressions. Ask for forgiveness for areas in which you have not hallowed His name in your life and ask to be given a new beginning. He will guide you, for it is what the Lord Jesus Himself taught His disciples to pray: our father who art in heaven, hallowed be thy name.

Let His name be hallowed. In His name, there is healing. In His name, there is salvation. In His name, there is restoration of the soul, body, and spirit. In His name, there is deliverance; there is protection in His name. His name is a strong tower that the righteous run into and are safe; therefore, His name is a refuge. Let His name be hallowed, for in that name, there is resurrection. Father, You are in heaven, hallowed be thy name.

Take a moment and reflect on your own life and ask God that His name may be hallowed in your daily life and in the lives of your immediate and extended family. I have realized through experience that when I finally surrender and let the Lord have His way—and unfortunately, many a time, it comes as a *finally*—I find that I have peace and less anxiety. Let God's name be hallowed in your daily life. He loves you, and the plans He has for you are for good and not for evil. He is watching all over the earth to show Himself mighty and powerful on your behalf because you love Him. Hallowed be Thy name, oh Lord.

Prayer for this section:

Heavenly Father, thank You for this section of the Lord's Prayer that says, "Hallowed be thy name." Help me in my daily walk such that in the words that proceed out of my mouth, in the thoughts that I entertain in my mind, and in the behaviors with which I portray myself and You, I let Your name be hallowed.

Whenever I communicate both verbally and nonverbally, when I am at work, at home, with strangers, or with family and friends, let Your name be hallowed. Whenever I am in need and searching for answers, let Your name be hallowed. In the prayer requests that I present to You and as You answer them, Lord, let Your name be hallowed.

Sometimes I become anxious and do not know what to do, and sometimes I am filled with fear; lead me so that Your name may be hallowed, dear Father. Sometimes I have hurt people in the way I speak to them, and it does not hallow Your name. Help me to be conscious in what I say, where I go, and what I do that Your name may be hallowed.

I surrender all to You, my blessed heavenly Father. As long as Your name is hallowed in everything, it shall be well with my soul. I thank You that Your name is a strong tower, and when I run to it, I am safe. I am grateful that the name of Jesus is the name that we were given, a name that is above every situation, above every sickness and disease, a name that has unceasing power and every principality. I thank You for the privilege of Your great name and the unceasing power of Your name. May that name be hallowed.

CHAPTER 3

Thy Kingdom Come

After hallowing the Father's name, we are to pray that His kingdom come and be established here on earth. To ask that His "kingdom come" is to acknowledge that the kingdom is already established elsewhere, and we are now asking that it can be established here on earth as well.

I would like us to bear in mind that during this time of Jesus's ministry on earth, the Israelites were used to being ruled by kingdoms that had conquered them. At this time, they were ruled by the Romans. Due to the oppression that they went through, and given the knowledge that they were God's chosen people historically, God's kingdom would be a better kingdom. So according to the many prophecies that the Jewish people had heard for a long time, they believed that Jesus was going to be an earthly king who would conquer their oppressors and build a strong Jewish kingdom. They saw Jesus as their own king who would redeem them. They failed to understand that Jesus's kingdom was not an earthly kingdom.

In order to fully understand this part, it is important to define what is meant by the kingdom. A kingdom is a territory, a nation. or a country that is ruled by a king or queen. In every kingdom, there are subjects of the king or queen, most of whom

– 24 –

Thy Kingdom Come

are born in that country or become citizens by a process called naturalization. For example, I was born and raised in Kenya. I moved to the United States as an immigrant and became a citizen by naturalization. Every kingdom on earth has boundaries and rules that govern that kingdom. There are regulations by which the people ought to abide, and every kingdom is different and unique because of them.

There are benefits that citizens of that kingdom can enjoy but foreigners cannot. The citizens of that country must live by the law of the land. When the laws are not followed, that is a violation. We know that no king will allow another king to rule his kingdom. That is why, for example, for the case of the US, after a new president has been sworn in, the former president moves out of the White House and paves the way for the new president to move in. After the transition is complete, the new king or president is now able to execute his leadership.

The people in that kingdom or country must abide by the rule of the new king. Whoever lives in that country or kingdom must abide by the law of the land. For example, if a person moves from the United States to Britain, they must live by the rules of the British government. They won't say, "Oh, in my country, we do it *this* way or *that* way, and *that* is the way I am going to do it." They have to live by the law of that kingdom or country. If the citizens drive on the right side of the road, that is what the newcomer is going to abide by. If they don't, they will be going against the law of the land and may face consequences.

I would like us to understand that during this time, the Jewish people were under Roman rule. In their minds, they were happy that when God's kingdom comes, they will be free from the rule and oppression of the Romans. That is why they thought that Jesus was an earthly king. I believe that they waited for Him to take over the kingdom, and there are instances when they wanted to make Him ruler over them, but on some occa-

The Secret and Power of Praying the Lord's Prayer

sions, He disappeared. We see one incident as recorded in the gospel of John 6:15, "Therefore when Jesus realized that they were about to come and take Him by force and make Him king, He withdrew again to a mountain by himself alone."

If you remember, in Acts 1:6, the Bible says the following: "Therefore, when they had come together, they asked Him, saying, 'Lord, will You at this time restore the kingdom to Israel?'" This is after Jesus has resurrected from the dead and He is about to return to heaven, but they are still seeing Him as their earthly king who was overdue in taking over the kingdom; now they are wondering if at this time after He has resurrected, He will do what, to them, He was supposed to have done a long time ago.

Now when Jesus taught the disciples to pray, "Your kingdom come," He was teaching them to pray, "God, You rule over us, and we will be Your subjects. We are willing to welcome Your kingdom and all that pertains to it. Whatever the rule, whatever the requirement, we are willing to let Your kingdom come. When Your kingdom comes, we will be Your subjects, and You will reign in us. You are king, and Your rule is allowed to reign in our lives."

Let's talk about the days of colonial rule. Most countries in Africa were ruled or colonized by other countries. For example, my country of birth, Kenya, was colonized by the British. Kenya gained her independence in 1963, which was before I was born. When a country colonized another country, the colonized country has to change the way it does things to reflect the country that is colonizing her. Everything, even the educational system, must change in the colony. Governors are appointed in accordance with the rule of the colonizer.

The story of the prophet Daniel and his Hebrew friends, recorded in Daniel 3:1–16, would be a good illustration of this. This book says that per the order of King Nebuchadnezzar, several Hebrew boys were to be fed the king's food, taught the lan-

– 26 –

Thy Kingdom Come

guage for three years, then brought to serve in the king's palace. That meant that in order for them to be able to serve the king, they needed to be taught and fed according to the customs of that kingdom. At the end of it, they will have adapted to the lifestyle of that unfamiliar kingdom.

When we pray that the Lord's kingdom come, we commit to learning the laws of the kingdom and show that we are willing to follow them to the letter by His grace. Learn and feed on the Word of God to know the kingdom rules and regulations. This will mean that we intentionally spend time in prayer and the studying of the Word. As we say, "Let your kingdom come," we are causing His kingdom to come through our speech, actions, relationships, and conduct. Let His kingdom come into our lives. There is no way for two kings to rule together. Just as Jesus said in Matthew 6:24, you cannot serve two Masters; you will either obey one and disobey the other.

The question here is this: in your day-to-day life, as you interact with people and hang out with your friends and loved ones, what kingdom is mostly seen? Is it the kingdom of God or the kingdom of darkness? Whose kingdom is seen in the words which come out of your mouth?

There is no such thing as a scanner that automatically identifies if someone is a Christian. The world will tell you apart by your words, actions, and overall behaviors. We have a mandate to let God's kingdom come in our daily lives. We must be willing to deliberately let go of the former kingdom and its leadership and way of life in order for God's kingdom to fully come. We each have to look within ourselves and identify ways in which we have been pushing against the kingdom of God coming into our lives. Is it by a lying tongue? Is it through backbiting or cursing? Have we been unfaithful, disobedient, or envious? Is it grudge-holding, unforgiveness, or pride? Is it fornication or adultery?

The Secret and Power of Praying the Lord's Prayer

May the Lord help you as you search yourself. As the Holy Spirit reveals to you the areas where you have resisted the kingdom of God, repent and ask for forgiveness. The Holy Spirit is our teacher and counselor. God is faithful. He knows you cannot do it alone. Ask for help and be honest and pray, acknowledging that you cannot overcome your sin alone. He will help you and strengthen you.

Prayer for this section:

Father, in Jesus's name, I have learned this section of the Lord's Prayer, "let Your kingdom come." I have realized that there are ways in which I have not portrayed Your kingdom in my daily life. I have had times I have been involved in things I should not be involved in as Your child and a follower of Jesus Christ.

I pray Thee, oh Father, that You forgive me and cleanse me with the blood of Jesus. Help me to be conscious and to purpose to follow Your Word. The Bible tells me that You are the one who gives me the power both to do and to will for Your good pleasure. May You give me the strength to do my part so that Your kingdom may come in my daily life. I am so used to doing things my own way, and sometimes, it doesn't reflect Your kingdom. Help me, oh Lord, my Rock, my strength, and my redeemer. In Jesus's name I pray. Amen.

CHAPTER 4

Thy Will Be Done on Earth As It Is in Heaven

The word *will* is used quite frequently in our day-to-day conversations. We say, "I will come to see you tomorrow," "He will not go to work today," "I will be glad if you come to my soccer game." We also use the word *will* when we talk about death. Whenever you go to the hospital, you are asked if you have a "living will." This is a document that one has written, expressing what he or she wants to happen in case there reaches a time when he/she is unable to make decisions or what must happen to his property at the time of his death. For example, someone may leave their house to their children or designate money to a charity or church organization, and so forth.

I work in health care, and I have cared for people during their last days of their lives. I have seen some cases where, according to the dying patient's written will—which may not be known to the children, depending on the relationship they had with the parent, for example if the child did not treat them well—things turn in a very bad way for that son or daughter. At the deathbed of the patient, while the child is hoping to inherit everything, the parent's will states something quite different. The will is always followed to the letter. Some people have

– 29 –

received an inheritance from someone's will that they never expected; all they are told is that the *will* stated that they receive a certain amount of money or property.

Another place where the will is used is after a general election. The politicians say that the will of the people has been done. We have had good and bad things happen to people because of a collective will.

This section of the Lord's Prayer goes, "Your will be done on earth as it is in heaven." I want to begin by recalling what the Bible tells us about the creation of man. Man was made from the soil: "And the LORD God formed man of the dust of the ground and breathed into his nostrils the breath of life; and man became a living being" (Genesis 2:7). He became a living being after the breath of God poured into his nostrils. That means that without the breath of God in man's nostrils, he is simply dirt.

This is a crucial point to note. Man was not a living being; he was simply a pile of dirt put together in the same way a cup or pot shaped from clay by a potter. That is why, without the breath of God in us, we are nothing but bodies. Therefore, when Jesus said, "Thy will be done on earth as it is in heaven," *earth* can refer to the person; I want to use this meaning. We were made from the earth. We pray that God's will be done in our lives as it is done in heaven.

Knowing this concept and knowing His will for our lives are of paramount importance. What does the Bible teach about our daily lives? There are many areas in the Scriptures where we see God expressing His will for us or, in other words, expressing His requirements for leading a godly life.

We read this in the book of Romans: "If it is possible, as much as depends on you, live peaceably with all men" (Romans 12:18). Living at peace with friends is very easy to do, but it is a whole different story when it comes to people who have hurt

Thy Will Be Done on Earth As It Is in Heaven

you, especially when some of them still do things that hurt you. For those people who you feel is incredibly hard to love, ask for the grace of God. Be honest and tell Him that it is hard for you to love them. Ask for His strength to enable you. Do all you can. Choose to do the hard thing; it would be easy to block them on your phone contacts or even try to get even with them, but the hard thing is often what will be pleasing to God, living at peace with all men.

Paul writes,

> I beseech you therefore, brethren, by the mercies of God, that you present your bodies as a living sacrifice, holy, and acceptable to God, which is your reasonable service. And do not be conformed to this world, but be transformed by the renewing of your mind, that you may prove what is good and acceptable and perfect will of God. (Romans 12:1–2)

Here, Paul is talking of how we can come to know the will of God. It is by doing these things: first, we live at peace with all people; second, we offer our bodies as a living sacrifice to God; third, we do not conform to the patterns of the present world; and fourth, we seek to be transformed by the renewing of our minds. That way, we will be able to know the true and perfect will God has for us.

Another thing I have found very helpful in causing God's will to be done in my life is giving a sacrifice of praise. This means praising even when I don't feel like it. This is not easy, especially when you have been waiting on a breakthrough that has shown no sign of coming; this is why it is called a *sacrifice* of praise, as recorded in Hebrews 13:15, saying, "Therefore by

The Secret and Power of Praying the Lord's Prayer

Him let us continually offer the sacrifice of praise to God, that is, the fruit of *our* lips, giving thanks to His name."

This is why faith is the substance of things hoped for, the evidence of things not seen. Feelings are like visitors; they come, and at some point, they go, or they change. Praise God for who He is, and if you have seen a breakthrough in the past, praise God for it and trust Him; remember young king David when he was facing the philistine giant, Goliath? The Bible says, "Moreover David said, 'The LORD, who delivered me from the paw of the lion and from the paw of the bear, He will deliver me from the hand of this Philistine.'" And Saul said to David, "Go, and the LORD be with you!" (1 Samuel 17:37). We must say like we mean it and like we have confidence that God is the same yesterday and today and forever. David remembered that if God was able to give him victory yesterday, then He is able to give him victory today. Praise Him on credit. You will be amazed at how the heavy burden will be lifted from your heart as you surrender, saying, "God, I don't understand, but I praise you, for *you* understand, and nothing comes to me accidentally."

We want to know the will of God in countless areas of our lives. We ask our pastors, prayer warriors, and friends to pray that we may know the will of God. I have prayed this on many occasions. In many prayer meetings, when it is time to pray for each other's needs, I have said, "Pray that I may know the will of God for my life in this certain area of my life." I am sure that I am not alone. Maybe you or someone you know has asked for that kind of prayer.

But the real question is this: how willing are we to do His will once we know it? This point cannot be overstated as when praying for a life partner. I know many of us have been in this, me included. You see a nice young man/woman. You feel he/she is the right one for you. You go into prayer, asking God for a life partner, and you say, "Please, please, please, God, let it be Allan/

Thy Will Be Done on Earth As It Is in Heaven

Jane," naming the person you feel in love with at the moment. You get super excited when you read a text message from him/her (I am not saying that everyone you might feel to be your partner is wrong).

With time, things start changing. The excitement is dying down. You no longer feel the same way you felt at first. You start saying, "Maybe he/she is not the one." Many times, it is after you have cooled down that you start seeing the flaws in the person, and now you are able to say, "Hmm, I don't think I can stand this or that." At that point, you can now pray for God to help you find the right one for you. Can we be honest that if God indeed answered our prayers during our high moments, we could only have ourselves to blame? Are you happy that God sometimes does not answer our prayers exactly how we want Him to answer? It takes humility and surrender to ask for God's will, know it, and obey it.

The Word of God is the mind of God, and God has expressed to us what He expects of us. I would like you to ask yourself these questions and write them down: First, what are some instances where you have tried to live at peace with all people, and what are the challenges you have encountered in doing so? Second, what are some of the ways in which you have offered your body as a living sacrifice unto God, and what are some of the ways you have failed to do so? Third, what are some of the ways in which you have conformed to the patterns of this nature and some of the ways that you have been able to not conform? And fourth, what are some of the ways in which you have been able to renew your mind—hence, transforming your life?

In all of these, write down how reading this scripture has shed some light on your spiritual man so that you can cause God's will to be done in your life as it is in heaven. I recommend going through your Bible and finding every scripture that talks about the will of God and write each one down. Refer to

– 33 –

The Secret and Power of Praying the Lord's Prayer

and read them regularly. I am sure the Word will start transforming you, letting His will be done on earth (in your life) as it is in heaven.

Letting someone's will be done is not a simple or easy thing. I am sure you can remember a time when you wanted to do things a certain way, and your parents wanted you to do it a different way. Maybe you wanted to hang out with your friends a little longer, but your parents wanted you home.

At your work, your boss or manager—especially a new manager—wants things done one way, and perhaps you are used to doing things a different way. How does that feel? There are times when a new manager causes a shift in procedure so drastic that long-term employees cannot stand it and some of them quit their jobs. This is an example of letting someone else's will be done.

We all know that letting someone's will be done in your life is not a smooth ride. It can bring lots of friction, be it at home with children or spouses or at work. It takes lots of humility, trust, and surrender to let someone else's will be done in your life.

I would like you to take a moment and reflect on areas in your early life, at work, or in your relationships where you had to make accommodations for another person's will. What did it feel like on the inside? How did those feelings affect your demeanor, attitude, or mood? If you ended up accepting the will of that person, what did it cost you on a daily basis, and for how long did you struggle with adjusting to their will? I believe that this is why you often find many people holding grudges or resenting someone because of a "strong will." It is a my-way-or-the-highway mentality. It takes humility, trust, and surrender for one to be able to let another person's will be done.

Jesus taught His disciples humility, trust, and surrender as necessary qualities for being children of God. He not

Thy Will Be Done on Earth As It Is in Heaven

only taught them these qualities, but He demonstrated them throughout His life here on earth, the final example being in the garden of Gethsemane. "He went a little farther and fell on His face and prayed, saying, 'O My Father, if it is possible, let this cup pass from Me; nevertheless, not as I will, but as You will'" (Matthew 26:39). He made His needs known unto the Father but was humble enough to surrender and let the Father's will be done. He also reminded his disciples as illustrated in the following scripture about doing the Will of God the father: "But why do you call Me 'Lord, Lord,' and not do the things which I say" (Luke 6:46)? "For whoever does the will of My Father in heaven is My brother and sister and mother" (Matthew 12:50). "Not everyone who says to Me, 'Lord, Lord,' shall enter the kingdom of heaven, but he who does the will of My Father in heaven" (Matthew 7:21). In His last words before He died, Christ surrendered His Spirit to the Father, as recorded in Luke 23:46: "And when Jesus had cried out with a loud voice, He said, 'Father, into Your hands I commit My spirit.' Having said this, He breathed His last."

Once the kingdom of God has been allowed into our lives, once we have let God be king over our everyday lives, His will may be done in our lives as it is in heaven. It means that God is taking control and leadership and that His people are walking in the Spirit so that they don't gratify the desires of the flesh. Paul writes this:

> Walk in the Spirit, and you shall not fulfill the lust of the flesh. For the flesh lusts against the Spirit, and the Spirit against the flesh; and these are contrary to one another, so that you do not do the things that you wish. (Galatians 5:16–17)

Walking in the Spirit is what brings the will of God to be done in our lives. This chapter of Galatians points out what the fruit of the Spirit is and what the lust of the flesh looks like.

In order for us to have the will of God done in our lives as it is done in heaven, we must know the will of God and be humble enough to surrender our wills to His will. We must understand that sometimes, it is painful to let His will be done. It is easier to just follow our feelings and seek what is comfortable in the moment than to humble ourselves. It is going to take determination, like Paul says, "I discipline my body like an athlete, training it to do what it should. Otherwise, I fear that after preaching to others I myself might be disqualified" (1 Corinthians 9:27).

To discipline someone is easier than to discipline yourself because you are the one who feels the want, and you are the one who has to endure the pain of the discipline. It is called self-discipline. By studying the Word of God and spending time in prayer, we will know the will of God for our daily lives. Self-discipline, time spent studying the Word, and praying will help us to stay closer to God. We can then be humble enough to let Him have His way in our lives. If not, what would be the point of saying, "His will be done in us as it is in heaven," if we don't know it or we are not ready to let him lead us His way? It is like a child asking its mom, "How can I help in the kitchen?" Once he/she is told what to do, he/she doesn't take any pains in doing a thing about it.

Jesus said, "If you know these things, blessed are you if you do them" (John 13:17). This means that it is not only important to know the will of God, but it is more important to do what you know to be the right thing.

Thy Will Be Done on Earth As It Is in Heaven

Prayer for this section:

Father, in Jesus's name, thank You for this section of surrender, praying that Your will may be done in my life as it is in heaven. As much as it is my desire to always pray that I may know Your will in my life, time and time again, I find myself fixated on my own desires, and self-will tends to overtake me, and I find it hard to do that which I know to be Your will.

Without You, I am not able to know Your will, let alone doing it and letting it be done in my life as it is in heaven. I pray Thee today that by the help of the Holy Spirit, who is my teacher and counselor, You help me to be more conscious of what I do and the choices I make so that Your will may be done in me as it is in heaven.

Your will is bigger than my will, for Yours encompasses the present and the future. Where there is a conflict of wills between mine and Yours, please help me to quickly surrender so that Yours may be done. When I am looking for a spouse or a job, buying a home, help me to listen to the small voice of the leading of the Holy Spirit, who says, "This is the way. Walk in it." When I am anxious and desperate, help me trust and know that You have my best interest at heart and that nothing happens to me accidentally, for I am Your child. Help, dear Lord to let Your will be done in all my offices in this life. Sometimes I struggle in doing your will in my daily life. As Paul said in Romans 7:19, 21–25:

> *For the good that I will to do, I do not do;*
> *but the evil I will not to do, that I practice.*
> *I find then a law, that evil is present with*
> *me, the one who wills to do good. For I delight*
> *in the law of God according to the inward man.*
> *But I see another law in my members, warring*
> *against the law of my mind, and bringing me*

The Secret and Power of Praying the Lord's Prayer

> *into captivity to the law of sin which is in my members. O wretched man that I am! Who will deliver me from this body of death? I thank God—through Jesus Christ our Lord!*

I need Your help to do Your will, Lord, for only with Your can I make it. Thank You in advance. In Jesus's name I pray. Amen.

CHAPTER 5

Give Us This Day Our Daily Bread

When the Israelites journeyed through the wilderness, there came a time when they ran out of the food they had carried with them from Egypt. They were worried about what they were going to eat, given the fact that they were in the wilderness. Without food, they knew that they were not going to last long. They complained to Moses and Aaron:

> In the desert the whole community grumbled against Moses and Aaron. The Israelites said to them, "If only we had died by the Lord's hand in Egypt! There we sat around pots of meat and ate all the food we wanted, but you have brought us out into this desert to starve this entire assembly to death." Then the Lord said to Moses, "I will rain down bread from heaven for you. The people are to go out each day and gather enough for that day." (Exodus 16:1–4)

Here we see God providing them with their daily bread. Bread was a staple food for the Israelites; when the Lord said

The Secret and Power of Praying the Lord's Prayer

this portion of the prayer, He was using what the Hebrew people were used to.

The timing is very important as we look and dig through this prayer. It comes after the hallowing of God's name and humbling of spirit. The disciple's hearts have now been so inclined unto their heavenly Father that they will need to ask for daily bread, the life sustainer.

See that Jesus did not tell them to start with asking for their daily bread. Many times, we start our prayers with something like a shopping list for God to grant, and that is sometimes all we do. We name what we want for ourselves, our loved ones, and occasionally, what others want. But following this example of Jesus, the asking of our daily bread comes closer to the end than the beginning. This was for a reason. Worshiping God must precede asking for our needs and wants, not the other way round.

We know that food alone does not give life, but it is necessary sustenance for life. In other words, those who are alive will always need food to sustain their lives. They need it for strength, building and repairing worn-out cells and tissues, and for disease fighting and prevention, as well as other things. Food is necessary as long as one is alive. However, those who are dead do not need food. Therefore, no matter what food you present to them, they will not eat and do not need the food. Let us remember this point: that after they had accepted Jesus to be their Lord and Savior, Jesus's disciples needed daily bread to sustain them spiritually. Jesus knew this.

As we all know, whatever you feed will grow, and whatever is not fed will eventually die. The need for daily bread is a natural, basic need for all living things, including humans. The disciples knew that they could ask God the Father for the provisions that were very important; they knew that it was the will of the Father to provide them with their daily bread. I will

Give Us This Day Our Daily Bread

talk about the general benefits we get from bread. I don't mean literal bread; I am looking at food in general.

Food is grouped into different categories. There are foods that give us energy, those that help repair worn-out tissues, and those that help us fight against diseases and germs. This means that following recommended nutritional guidelines, we eat a balanced diet that allows our bodies to function as they are supposed to. That is why nutritional guidelines give us a daily amount of each food category we should eat. Without the guidelines, many people would concentrate on the sweet foods that taste good and would not touch other foods that do not taste as good.

I think we all can remember a time when Mom tried to push some foods, especially green beans, but all the children, even the youngest baby, resisted the beans because of their bad taste. However, Mom continued to push for the beans until the kids accepted that they needed to eat them. Vegetables are not popular with many children, but Mom knows what is important for her children's health.

Naturally, we know that we must eat daily. There is a range from those who eat a meal a day to those who have three meals a day; some even add snacks as well. But the bottom line is that under normal circumstances, we all need to eat daily for nourishment.

If the Lord meant only physical food, it would be hard to present this prayer to those who have plenty in their lives. How do you tell someone who grew up with plenty to pray, "Give us this day our daily bread"? Such a person has probably never lacked food, clothing, or shelter. It is difficult for such a person to understand this section. How do you ask for God to give you your daily bread when you already have more than enough?

This is why I am convinced that the Lord Jesus was not necessarily talking about the physical food we need for our daily

The Secret and Power of Praying the Lord's Prayer

livelihood. If that were the case, then it could only be applicable to the poor and less privileged. I want to believe that the Lord meant more than the physical food we eat daily. If indeed Jesus meant for this prayer to be the model for His disciples' daily prayers, then He must have meant more than the physical need for nutritional intake. All must be able to pray this section of the Lord's Prayer, not just those who have a need for bread, not just those who lack. That's why I believe it denotes more than just ordinary daily bread.

Without proper nutrition, our bodies will be weak and prone to diseases. That is why it is important to fight against hunger and starvation. When people, especially children, lack certain kinds of foods, their growth and development can be affected; babies can fail to thrive due to lack of necessary nutritional nutrients.

Let us look at the significance of bread in the biblical Hebrew culture. We remember that during the exodus from Egypt, God rained bread down from heaven in the wilderness. "And God said to Moses, 'Behold, I will rain bread from heaven for you, and the people will go out and gather'" (Exodus 16:4). The audience that Jesus was talking to about this prayer knew the history of a time when their ancestors were in the wilderness, as they journeyed from Egypt to Canaan under the leadership of Moses, and how God provided bread from heaven, as recorded in the book of Exodus. According to these passages (Exodus 16:1–36 and Numbers 11:1–9), they knew that God could provide as He did for their ancestors.

Bread is used even in our daily lives. We always refer to the one who works to bring home an income as the *breadwinner* of the home. I have heard people express devastation at funerals many times when they state that the deceased was the only breadwinner and wonder who the family is going to depend on now that he or she is no more. Bread is a symbol of food, the one thing that we all need. In our day-to-day lives, the bread-winner is the income earner. That shows us how important bread is to our lives.

But the New Testament takes it to a whole new level, a confusing one to many in the audience. We see Jesus telling them that He is the bread of life in John 6:35, 48, and 58. Jesus is saying that He is our daily bread. As we already know, bread is important to our bodies. We know that food helps build and repair worn-out tissues and cells of our bodies. It also provides energy so we can do our work. It also helps our bodies to fight against diseases and germs. Without food, we will be weak, prone to infections, and may die. We all know when to eat; most of us have scheduled mealtimes. People's mealtimes range from one meal a day to five meals a day, snacks included. I believe that Jesus wasn't worried that His disciples would lack food; they needed to ask for it from God. He had more He was intending for them to know about this part of the prayer than physical nutrition.

Let's see what happened to Jesus after He was baptized. He was led into the wilderness to be tempted by the devil. After being in the wilderness for forty days and night, Jesus was hungry. The first temptation Satan gave Him was to turn stones into bread, if indeed He was the Son of God. I want us to look at Jesus's answer as recorded in Matthew 4:4: "But He answered and said, 'Man shall not live by bread alone, but by every word that proceeds from the mouth of God.'" We need to know that Jesus was quoting directly from the book of Deuteronomy, which says,

> He humbled you, allowed you to hunger and then fed you with manna, which you did not know, nor did your fathers know, that he might make you know that man shall not

The Secret and Power of Praying the Lord's Prayer

live by bread alone, but man lives by every word that proceeds from the mouth of God. (Deuteronomy 8:3)

Before we connect all these together, let us also consider the scripture that says,

In the beginning was the word, and the word was with God, and the word was God. He was in the beginning with God. All things were made through Him, and without Him nothing was made that was made. (John 1:1–3)

These scriptures above have said, "Man shall not live by bread alone, but by every word that proceeds from the mouth of God." Also, the Word is referring to Jesus Christ. Now, in this portion of the Lord's Prayer, Jesus is the bread that He is telling them to ask for. It is the Word that He is telling them to ask for in their prayers. Give us this day our daily portion of Your Word.

I believe He was telling them that because He is the bread of life, they may ask to get a daily portion of Him who is the Word. This means that it is not a one-time dose of Jesus or the Word and we are done but a daily portion of Jesus or the Word in our lives. Jesus is saying that He is our daily bread. It is a daily commitment. Not a once-a-week portion, not a once-a-month bread, not a once-a-year kind of bread, but a daily bread. And again, I say daily bread. This means reading, meditating, and living the Word on a daily basis. That's our spiritual bread.

Just as we need physical food daily, we need the Word of God daily, which is our spiritual food. When we get our daily bread, which is the Word of God, it will do in our spiritual lives what food does in our physical bodies. It will give us strength

Give Us This Day Our Daily Bread

to do what the Lord wants us to do; it will give us strength to overcome temptation; it will help us grow closer to God. It will repair our broken and worn-out spiritual tissues. It will help us to testify of the great works of our Lord and Savior Jesus Christ. Therefore, Lord, give us this day a portion of the Lord Jesus who is the bread of life.

When we are hungry, we get food. When we are weak, we know food will strengthen us. When we are injured, we are encouraged by the doctor to eat certain foods that help repair our worn-out tissues. When we go to the doctor and our blood levels are checked, we are advised to either increase, decrease, or totally eliminate consumption of certain foods from our diet, depending on the doctor's recommendations. For example, I work as a nurse, so I am familiar with different kinds of foods and what their consumption might cause in the human body. For example, if one gets diagnosed as having diabetes, they will be advised to watch their carbohydrates and sugar intake as part of their treatment plan. According to what ails us, the doctor will advise us on our food intake. Someone with high blood pressure will be advised to limit salt and other foods to manage it. Food is so important that even when people have differences and they want to reconcile, they will share a meal together. When we have done something good, we have a party to celebrate the achievement, and guess what we do? We eat together.

I am not saying that Jesus did not mean for the disciples to ask for physical bread. What I am saying here is that it is not only physical food that they were to ask for. What I am trying to help us understand is that the Lord Jesus was concerned with more than physical bread.

The Lord, who is the bread of life, tells us to ask for Him to give us a daily portion of Jesus, the Word. He knew that when we ask for a daily portion of Jesus, whom the Bible actually refers to as the bread of life, we will have the strength to do the

– 45 –

will of the Father, the strength to overcome sin and temptation, courage when we face discouraging moments, and hope when we face hopeless situations. A daily portion of Jesus in our lives will enable us to walk in the Spirit so that we won't gratify the desires of the flesh. Therefore, Father, give this day our daily bread.

As we look into the Word of God, I can't help but think of times that I have just opened the Bible, and the Word just speaks to my very situation. It comes like a glass of cold water to my thirsty soul. One of the many times that I can remember is way back after high school. I was working for a small private company back in Kenya. Being the only employee of a poor company, I was not paid monthly as I was supposed to.

For those familiar with Kenya, we are not an industrialized country, so getting a job is not easy. I therefore said to myself, as long as I have food and shelter, I can wait until he pays me. It wasn't that we did not make money, but the guy had his own things to do that he felt were pressing, and paying me was secondary. It was in one of those moments of stress and uncertainty, not knowing when he will pay me, that I was asking God many questions. I opened the Bible to Revelation 3:8. It said, "I know your works. See, I have set before you an open door, and no one can shut it. For you have a little strength, have kept my word and have not denied my name."

While I was a very young believer, the man I was working for was a mature Christian. However, I felt that he was doing the wrong thing by not paying me. He was concerned with his own needs. That scripture spoke directly to my situation, and I have lived by it. I believe that I have lived to see that open door, and I believe that I am still yet to see more. I need to continue trusting in Him. That word was my bread for that day.

I do not know if you can think of a time when Scripture or a person spoke to you and the encouragement was all you needed to go through that day, but as Scripture says,

> Every scripture is given by inspiration of God, and is profitable for doctrine, for reproof, for correction, and for instruction in righteousness, that the man of God may be complete, thoroughly equipped for every good work. (2 Timothy 3:16–17)

This is another section that shows us that when we have the Word, we are equipped for every good work. We will need this daily, and it is Jesus who is the bread of life.

Just as natural life cannot be sustained if we do not eat, our spiritual lives cannot be sustained without a daily portion of Jesus. Our spiritual lives will be weakened without the Word, and if we stay long without a daily portion of Jesus, we will be spiritually stagnant and eventually die spiritually.

Prayer for this section:

Heavenly Father, I thank You for this portion of the Lord's Prayer. I pray today that You give me this day my daily bread. Give me a daily portion of Your Word that can speak to my situation right now, in Jesus's name.

When I am happy or when I am sad, when I am sick, or when I am well, give me a daily portion of Your Word that brings healing. When I am anxious, give me a portion of Your Word that tells me not to be anxious for anything but that in everything, by prayer and supplication, I can make my requests known unto You and that Your peace, which surpasses all my understanding, will guard my heart and mind through Christ Jesus.

The Secret and Power of Praying the Lord's Prayer

Give me a daily portion of You, such that when I am facing a crossroad and I do not know which way to turn, the daily portion of Your Holy Spirit will whisper to me and tell me, "This is the way, walk in it" (Isaiah 30:21). Give me my daily portion of Your Word that assures me not to fear, for You are with me, that You will never leave me nor forsake me (Isaiah 41:10). When those who rise up against me are increasing and their plans to trap me feel imminent, give me my daily bread of Your Word that assures me that You are my strong and fortified tower that I run to and in which I find my safety (Proverbs 18:10).

When I reach a point where I feel worthless, less than enough, less than deserving, that no one cares, and that no one loves me, give me my daily bread that reminds me that You are concerned with everything that concerns me (1 Peter 5:7), that I am loved by You, that I am the apple of Your eye. As a single mother, when I feel that I am helpless, that I don't have enough money to feed my children, that I don't know where rent will come from—when many take advantage of me and my children and say that they will not succeed, for there is no one who will help me—give me Your daily Word that reminds me that You are the husband to the widows and a Father to the fatherless (Psalm 68:5), that I am Yours, and my children are Yours, that even as it is hard for me as a mother to forget my children at times, You will never forget me and them, that You have us in the palm of Your hands.

Thank You for being my daily bread that I need and cannot live without. Cause springs of living water to flow from within me and those that see me will see You, Jesus, who is alive in me. My hope for strength to overcome and to grow is in You, Lord Jesus.

Dear Father, I pray Thee, give me this day my daily bread in Jesus's name. Amen.

CHAPTER 6

And Forgive Us Our Trespasses As We Forgive Those Who Trespass against Us

When you hear the word *forgive*, what comes to your mind? Think about a time when you had done something really bad, and you knew that you had messed up big time. What feelings did you experience? Guilty feelings? Shameful feelings? Feelings of defeat, worthlessness? Maybe as a child, when those feelings came, you were afraid to face the person you had wronged. When you saw that person, you were very apologetic, and you asked them to forgive you.

If the person forgave you, there was a relief that came to you, and you felt free again. There are other times when people have had to ask for forgiveness for something for which they believe they are not guilty, but just for the sake of peace, they say, "Forgive me." I have been one of those who had to ask for forgiveness and apologize for something for which I was not in the wrong, but for the sake of peace and for the sake of my life, I pleaded to the person, saying, "Please forgive me." There are people who easily ask for forgiveness, and there are some who will never say, "I am sorry. Please forgive me." We also know

– 49 –

The Secret and Power of Praying the Lord's Prayer

some people who are easy to forgive and some who are not easily forgiven.

Forgive is a translation from the Latin language that means *pardon*. It means to consciously and deliberately release feelings of resentment or vengeance toward someone or a group of people who have harmed you, irrespective of whether they deserve it or not. They may have done it deliberately or unknowingly. It is something that you have to make a choice to do, and that choice is not an easy one because of the hurt they may have caused you.

I believe that you can remember a time when you were hurt by what someone did to you or said about you. Hurt can be physical or psychological. Some hurts leave a mark that can never be erased by time. For example, a robber breaks into your home and steals precious jewelry that no money can replace, or a molester molests you or your loved one, or a drunk driver hits you and takes the life of a loved one or disables you. All these and many more instances are real in our daily lives. Forgiving and forgetting is not so easy, is it? Let us see what the Lord exemplified in this section, "forgive us our trespasses as we forgive those who trespass against us."

The teaching here is that God's forgiveness of our trespasses or our wrongs is preceded by us forgiving those who trespassed against us. To illustrate forgiveness, Jesus told Peter a parable as recorded in Matthew 18:21–35. The interaction starts like this:

> Then Peter came to Him and said, "Lord, how often shall my brother sin against me, and I forgive him? Up to seven times?" Jesus said to him, "I do not say to you, up to seven times, but up to seventy times seven." (Matthew 18:21–23)

And Forgive Us Our Trespasses As We Forgive Those Who Trespass against Us

Jesus shows us in the parable that follows that we must forgive in order to be forgiven. There are instances recorded in the Bible where Jesus forgave, and the ultimate forgiveness was the last words He spoke as recorded in the Gospel according to Luke while hanging on the cross, saying, "Father, forgive them for they do not know what they are doing" (Luke 23:34). We see others like Stephen following this example when he was stoned by the people outside of the city. He also said the same words as Jesus did, as it is recorded in the book of Acts:

> And they stoned Stephen as he was calling on God and saying, "Lord Jesus, receive my spirit." Then he knelt down and cried out with a loud voice, "Lord, do not charge them with this sin." And when he had said this, he fell asleep. (Acts 7:59–60)

I would like us to take a pause and reflect on our own lives. Remember that person who did something unforgettably wrong to you? In other words, you cannot forgive them. What would it take for you to actually forgive that person? Not only does unforgiveness prevent us from being forgiven by God, but it puts us in bondage.

Think of a time you saw that person that you have not forgiven; think of the anger that rose within you. It didn't matter what you were doing at the moment; your peace was disturbed at seeing that person. You may have tried to hide it and continued to smile, but deep down in your heart, you were not at peace. Maybe the people with whom you were conversing noticed a change in your demeanor, and when asked, you told them there was nothing.

Forgiving is not easy. In fact, it is sometimes easier to forgive a stranger than a member of your own family. For example,

The Secret and Power of Praying the Lord's Prayer

a sister or brother may say something offensive to his or her sibling, and the latter might hold a grudge against his or her sibling. Whereas if the same was said by a girlfriend or boyfriend, it might be *no big deal.*

As I think about it, I realize that we are prone to remembering. Therefore, even after long periods of time, siblings and family members often remember things that were said or done, and the offensive events add up to make it a big deal, whereas a friend who may have done the same or said the same is off the hook. We do this because we expect our family to do better and to care more. We say, "They know me. They know what I like. Why would they do this to me?" We get offended when our expectations are not met. Can you think of a situation where you were not able to forgive your family, but it was easy to forgive a friend? What happened in the end?

Some things are easier said than done. When it is you who need to forgive, it is a different story. I have heard of a mom who ended up forgiving a driver who killed her son in a road accident. It is not an easy thing to do. And sometimes, people who are forgiven fail to forgive others. Remember the parable Jesus told His disciples about an unforgiving servant in the book of Matthew? We must forgive in order for us to be forgiven, but it does not come easy.

As much as it is a hard thing to forgive someone, it is the best thing we can do for ourselves. The unforgiveness we hold against someone often does us more harm than the person against whom we hold it. It happens that sometimes, the person is not even aware of the wrong they did to you. Have you been hurt by someone giving you the cold shoulder for a way you hurt them that you are not even aware of? I am sure it has happened to all of us. For example, someone says you gave her a look when you are totally innocent, or they say you behaved a certain way when you were not aware of it. Jesus knew that, in

And Forgive Us Our Trespasses As We Forgive Those Who Trespass against Us

this imperfect world of imperfect human beings, there is a need for forgiveness.

When someone truly asks for forgiveness, it usually comes from a genuine realization of the wrong they have done and a genuine remorse. There is a desire to mend the relationship. There are people who may not ask for forgiveness even if they wronged someone. It is hard for them to say, "I am sorry."

Also, to be able to forgive others of the mistakes they have made takes a lot of humility. It is not an easy thing to do. We are naturally prone to hold grudges and be judgmental. I believe that this is why this portion of the Lord's Prayer touches on two sides of forgiveness, connecting us to do our part in order to pave the way for God to forgive us our own sins.

Jesus not only taught this as a model prayer, but He demonstrated it during His life on earth in different areas, as recorded in the Holy Scriptures. For example, in the garden of Gethsemane, when His disciple severed the ear of the servant of the high priest when they came to arrest Jesus, Jesus rebuked the disciple and told him to put away his sword. Jesus did the hard thing of putting the servant's ear back. He also demonstrated forgiveness at the cross, as recorded in the Gospel according to Luke, when He cried, "Father, forgive them for they know not what they do" (Luke 23:34).

Many a time, we have no control of what people do to us or say about us, but we do have control over how we react to it. We want to forgive and not let our emotions get the best of us. It is not the easiest thing to do, but it is the best thing to do for ourselves. When we don't forgive, we become slaves of that wound of unforgiveness that we keep nursing. Forgiveness is for our own good so that God can also forgive us our sins. Unforgiveness will lead to bitterness and may lead to revenge. Man's anger does not produce the righteousness which God

The Secret and Power of Praying the Lord's Prayer

desires (James 1:20). He has told us in His Word that vengeance is His (Romans 12:19).

He who gave this sample prayer did it for us to observe and emulate. The main factor is that God's forgiveness of our sins is dependent on our forgiving those who have sinned against us, and He led by example. The Bible says in Philippians 2:13 that it is God who works in us both to will and to do for His good pleasure. When I read that scripture, I was encouraged; whatever I do that gives Him the glory, He is the one who will give not only the power to do it but also the willingness to do it. Praise His name. Amen.

I would like us to pause here and think deeply. Do you have someone who wronged you so badly that it is hard for you to forgive that person? Have you tried to let go, but it seems almost impossible? Is even the thought of forgiveness hurtful?

Know that you are not alone. The main point is that, according to the model prayer that our Lord Jesus taught His disciples to pray, for God to forgive us our trespasses, we must forgive those who trespass against us. Think about it; your forgiveness is tied to your also forgiving that person. Yes, I mean *that* one.

I ask that you make a decision to do the hardest thing: forgive that person. Ask God to enable you. Remind Him of His Word. Tell Him, "Father, You said that You are the one who gives me the power both to do and to will for Your good pleasure. Please give me that power now in order for me to forgive so-and-so, for without Your power, I cannot." I recommend that you just try Him now before you continue. I pray that you will experience that peace. He will strengthen you.

At this time, I feel like talking to you who have been holding hatred and grudge toward your mother/father for what they did or did not do. They failed to show you the right way. They

And Forgive Us Our Trespasses As We Forgive Those Who Trespass against Us

failed to provide for you. Maybe Dad or Mom walked away when you were young, and you never felt the love.

I would like you to take some deep thought on that. Could it be that they did that because they did not know any better? Could it be that while they were growing up themselves, they did not experience the love, and in a way, they were doing their best for you? You need to know that you can only give what you have. Maybe they failed to give you the love you deserved because they themselves did not have it.

Could you, by the mercies of God, forgive your parents? Try. It is hard, but it is doable. Those who have done the hard thing have found peace with themselves. You, too, can do it with God's help. Just do it. Would you?

Prayer for this section:

Father, in Jesus's name, I thank You for Your Word in this section that says that Your forgiveness of my sins is preceded by my forgiving those who have sinned against me.

Lord Jesus, You showed us by example how You forgave those who wronged You. On my own, I am unable to forgive, especially those who have hurt me physically, emotionally, and with all kinds of hurt. It pains me every time I think of their acts. At the same time, it is making me a slave of the hurt.

I pray Thee that You help me, dear Lord, so I can forgive them. It is hard for me, but Your Word says that You are the one who gives me the power both to do and to will for Your good pleasure and that nothing is too hard for You. I know with Your strength, I can forgive just as You forgave me through Christ Jesus. I choose to forgive so-and-so for the wrong she/he did to me/my family. May You forgive them Lord, for they did not know better.

CHAPTER 7

Lead Us Not into Temptation, but Deliver Us from Evil

Before we dive into what this section of the Lord's Prayer might mean, let us look at what the main verbs in this section are: *lead* and *deliver*. "To lead" means to cause someone or an animal to go with one by holding them by hand or to halter a rope while moving forward. It can also mean to guide. Depending on how it is used in a sentence, "to lead" can mean to map a route or means of access to a particular place in a particular direction. For example, one can say, "The double door leads to a long hallway," or by asking that question, lead to him revealing his secret.

Lead can also mean an initiative in an action for others to follow. An example could be, "The state is *leading* in the COVID-19 vaccines," or "It is leading in the rate of infections per day." We can talk of *lead* as in leading someone or a group of people. For example, we can say when referring to presidents as the world leaders, team leaders, or group leaders. The well-being or success of a group, team, or country, etc. depends on the kind of leader they have.

Having discussed the literal and daily meaning of the phrase "to lead," let us now connect the portion of the Lord's

Lead Us Not into Temptation, but Deliver Us from Evil

Prayer here. It says, "Lead us not into temptation." Let us connect what we have already known about leading into this part. When the disciples prayed to God to lead them not into temptation, the picture it creates in my mind is that of God holding their hands and walking with them. The other aspect of this is that there is a leader, who is God, and there are those who are led, and that is the disciples or us. God is not standing back and yelling to them. He is leading, guiding them, and walking with them every step of the way. He is the shepherd, and as the disciples were aware, a shepherd leads his flock, and the flock follows.

Jesus teaching them about God leading them was something that they were familiar with. As they walk with God's leading, they will not fear any evil, as the psalmist says in Psalm 23:4, "Yea, though I walk through the valley of the shadow of death, I will fear no evil; For You are with me; Your rod and Your staff, they comfort me." The disciples were being taught to always know that it is the Lord's leading that will give them the strength to overcome temptation—hence, lead us not into temptation.

It is even more true to me and you today than it was for the disciples during Jesus's time on earth. Evil is all around us, and without God's leading, we cannot stand. The Word says in the book of proverbs: "There is a way which seemeth right unto a man, but the end thereof are the ways of death." God is the one who will lead us to the right path that will not lead to death. He gives us the strength to withstand the works of the devil. The Bible says in the book of Philippians, "For it is God who works in you both to will and to do for *His* good pleasure" (Philippians 2:13). It is His pleasure to lead you and me. When we ask Him to lead us, we are asking Him to do what pleases Him.

The Secret and Power of Praying the Lord's Prayer

Let us now see the second part of this section, which says, "Deliver us from evil." We use the word *deliver* in our day-to-day communications. For example, we can say, "A delivery driver for UPS," or "He delivered a moving speech at the graduation that moved people into tears," or "She delivered a bouncing nine-pound baby boy." All these and many others are the ways you can think of that we use the word *deliver*.

"To deliver" someone may mean to rescue someone from something or someone. Many times, it is to rescue someone from harm or danger. This indicates that the person needing to be rescued cannot rescue themselves; they cannot deliver themselves. A deliverer must do it. This means that the one who is delivering the other must be stronger than the one who is being delivered or rescued, that the deliverer has access to some things or power or privileges that the one to be delivered does not.

For this section of the portion of the Lord's Prayer, we will look at two deliverers, one from the Old Testament and one from the New Testament. Let us remember the story of Moses. He was the child born to Hebrew parents and raised in the Egyptian king's palace as a prince. There came a time when God called Him to deliver the Israelites out of the bondage of the Egyptians. The book of Exodus in the Old Testament talks about how God used Moses to deliver the children of Israel. Other instances where *deliver* is used in the Old Testament is found in the book of Daniel. Here we see God's deliverance of Daniel from the den of lions. Daniel had a steadfast faith in his God no matter what happened as recorded in Daniel 6:12–28.

The other deliverance we see in the book of Daniel is of the Hebrew boys Shadrach, Meshach, and Abednego, men who worshiped and trusted their God so much that no threat would deter them from doing the right thing, which is to worship only one God, Yahweh (Daniel 3:8–25). Just like their friend Daniel, they had unwavering faith in God, so much faith that

Lead Us Not into Temptation, but Deliver Us from Evil

they would rather risk their own lives than worship other gods. In both the above cases, we see God delivering his faithful servants from the arm of their enemies. In both cases, the enemy was much greater than God's servants. But we see God showing himself mighty and powerful on their behalf. Praise God. He is the same yesterday, today, and forevermore. He will deliver us also. Let us trust Him even when it seems like we are facing a dead end. He makes a way where there is no way.

There are several instances in the Bible, both in the Old and New Testaments, where a deliverer is recorded. Moses is recorded and renowned in the Old Testament as a deliverer of God's people, Israel, from Egyptian bondage. Several scriptures record Moses as the deliverer of Israel; he rescued them from the danger of captivity, slavery, and bondage of the Egyptians.

The Bible talks of God leading them through the wilderness using Moses. Moses was known as the deliverer. After Moses, the Bible records other deliverers like Samson, who, from before he was conceived, was predestined to deliver the Israelites from the hands of the Philistines. There are many other deliverers recorded, many of whom are found in the book of Judges. Also, the book of Psalms is rich in scriptures where God delivers His servant David from all his enemies.

The greatest deliverer of all times is the Lord Jesus Christ. He is the Son of God, and from the time of conception, His purpose on earth was to deliver His people from their sins.

Now, with the understanding above, let us see this portion of the Lord's Prayer: lead us not into temptation but deliver us from evil. At this time of the Lord's Prayer, the disciples have acknowledged God as their Father, they have hallowed His name, and they have worshiped and humbled themselves for God's will to be done and His kingdom to come. They have also received a daily portion of Jesus, who is the bread of life. They are in communion with God.

–59–

The Secret and Power of Praying the Lord's Prayer

Now it is time to ask for the leading and deliverance they will need throughout their Christian lives. Jesus said, "I am the good shepherd." A good shepherd leads his sheep to the right place. Psalm 37:23 says; "The steps of a good man are ordered by the Lord and He delighteth in his ways." The Lord leads and guides His own. Psalm 23:2 says, "He makes me to lie down in green pastures; He leads me beside the still waters." This portion of the prayer is a way of surrender, saying, "Without you, we will be lost, will be tempted and might fall." Hence, He taught them to ask God the Father to "lead us not into temptation but deliver them from evil."

Jesus is teaching His disciples to pray that God might deliver or rescue them from evil. It is not a new thing for them because they know their history and how God delivered them from the hand of Pharaoh, how he used Samson, King David, and many others to deliver them from the Philistines. Jesus knew that like their forefathers were delivered from their enemies, they too can ask God to lead and deliver them.

Many a time, we pray for God to prevent us from hardships. But in this section of the Lord's Prayer and the examples we have seen above, God is not absent when we face hard testing. He is with us all the time. If we reach a point that we feel like asking, "If God is with me, why then is this happening to me? Why did He not prevent it from happening?" we can be assured that He not only prevents evil from happening, but He is also able to deliver.

Next time you find yourself in a situation that feels like a fiery furnace or a dark den of lions, remember the God who delivers. Call on Him. Ask Him to deliver you. Take a moment and ask yourself what areas of your life you see that you need God's deliverance from evil.

Prayer for this section:

Father in Jesus's name, thank you that you are my deliverer. I pray thee Lord that you may remind me that you are with me always. That even when I don't see you, even when I feel alone, and sometimes when I feel like the temptation is overwhelming, to know that you are there with me. Many times I pass through difficult times, sickness on me, my children, my loved ones, Lord, I need your deliverance. Like the Hebrew boys in the fiery furnace, sometimes my life feels like so, I pray that you deliver me oh Lord my rock and my strength. Sometimes I pass from one trial to the next, sometimes I feel like David who was running away from king Saul, help me know you are near and that you will never leave me nor forsake me for I have put my hope and trust in you. When I reach a place where I do not know which way to follow, face with crossroads, lead me to the right path, lead me not into temptation but deliver me from evil I pray thee. In Jesus's name, amen.

CHAPTER 8

Thine Is the Kingdom, the Power, and the Glory Forever and Ever. Amen.

The final part of the Lord's Prayer sums it all up. As the Lord Jesus comes to the final section of the prayer, which He taught His disciples to pray, we see the final surrender to God as they end the prayer; they have established their relationship with God as their Father, letting Him do what a good father does to his children, sometimes saying "yes," other times saying "wait," and even other times saying "no" to their requests. They have learned to accept the answers. They have hallowed the name of God in all their ways. They have allowed His kingdom to come into their daily lives. They let His will be done in their lives as it is in heaven. They have asked and received a daily portion of Jesus, who is the bread of life. By God's grace, they have forgiven those who trespassed against them, and they have let God lead them and have asked for Him to deliver them from evil.

It is now they have to realize that the kingdom and the power to do anything is God's, and all glory goes to God. That

Thine Is the Kingdom, the Power, and the Glory Forever and Ever. Amen.

is when they say, "Yours is the kingdom," and that means God is king over them, or in our day, He is the king over us.

We do as the king requires us to do. That calls for total obedience to the king. His is the kingdom. In His kingdom, there is patience, forgiveness, and love. His is the power, meaning that the power to do all things is His. He has the power to change things, but He never changes. Then finally, His is the glory, meaning He receives the glory after all is said and done. He does not share His glory with anyone. He is God above all.

Here, Jesus is reminding them or us that when we have been able to do great miracles and wonders in His name, we should always give glory to God. We should not take any glory, for we are just but vessels. Without Him, we can do nothing.

This is a great place for us to do a self-check here. I know many great men and women of God who were in ministry and were being used by God in mighty ways, but some of them fell into the trap of pride. They did not give God the glory due to Him; they took it upon themselves, and the Spirit of the Lord left them and are now working the works of the flesh. This should remind us to think back in the Old Testament in the book of Daniel, chapter 4, where King Nebuchadnezzar was taking all glory for how his kingdom was.

> Twelve months later, as the king was walking on the roof of the royal palace of Babylon, he said, "Is not this the great Babylon I have built as the royal residence, by my mighty power and for the glory of my majesty?"
>
> Even as the words were on his lips, a voice came from heaven, "This is what is decreed for you, King Nebuchadnezzar: Your royal authority has been taken from you. You

will be driven away from people and will live with the wild animals; you will eat grass like the ox. Seven times will pass by for you until you acknowledge that the Most High is sovereign over all kingdoms on earth and gives them to anyone he wishes.

All glory and honor belongs to God alone. I would say that even when you feel like people are praising you for a good work you are doing for the kingdom of God, be very conscious and purpose to return glory to God. Therefore, the power and the glory both now and forevermore belong to God and Him alone. Amen. This is the final surrender to God the Father.

CHAPTER 9

Practice Praying the Lord's Prayer

In this last section of the Lord's Prayer, I am going to pray as a sample prayer here. You could use this as a guideline to develop your own prayer, praying like the Lord taught His disciples. It may look like a summary, but I am trying to include every part we have learned from the beginning of this prayer. May it enrich your daily life and bring you closer to God the Father through His Son, our Lord and Savior, Jesus Christ. Amen.

My Father, I know that heaven is Your throne and the earth is Your footstool. I thank You for being my Father. You are a big God, but You also do not despise my small requests. Thank You because You can reach down and hear my prayer. Help me, Father, so that when You don't answer me as I ask, I would know that You are still working all things for my good. Sometimes when Your response is to wait, give me the strength to trust You and not give up.

As You answer my prayers, Lord, I know that You are able to give me exceedingly, abundantly above all that I can ask or think of because You love me, Your handmaiden. In the answers and solutions that I am looking and seeking for, may Your name be glorified. Let it be to Your glory so that even when others look at the way You have intervened, they will glorify Your mighty and holy name. In the deliverance, healing, salvation, and restoration of my loved ones, let Your name be glorified. Let men and women glorify You when they hear of Your mighty works upon the sons of men. There is power, wonder, working power in Your name that we can't even comprehend as humans. For in Your name, there is peace, joy, provision, restoration, reconciliation. Not only those, but at Your name, every knee will bow and every tongue will confess that Jesus is Lord to the glory of God the Father. Therefore, I pray Thee to let Your name be glorified.

You are my God and my King. Let Your kingdom come and Your will be done in my life as it is in heaven. Sometimes I have my own will as to how things should be done. But, dear Lord, I pray that where there is a conflict of wills, Yours be done, not mine. For Your will encompasses more than my will. Your will is greater than mine, for You know more of my future than I could remember my past. You know what is best for me because before I was formed in my mother's womb, You had known me, and before I was born, You had ordained. It is by Your will that I live and have my being. You have a perfect will for me to give me good and not evil. More than my earthly Father can give me what I ask for because sometimes, he is limited financially or limited with time to attend to all my needs. You are unlimited, and I know that You will do me good and not evil so that Your name may be glorified.

Jesus, You are the bread of life. Therefore, Father, give me a daily portion of Jesus, who is the bread of life. I do not pray for a one-time big portion, but may You give me daily portions so that I can have the strength to do Your will, that I may have the power to overcome sin. Just as our physical daily bread builds our bodies, gives us strength to work and also power to fight against diseases, a daily portion of Jesus will do the same in my spiritual life. He will build me up, giving me strength to do Your will and the power to

Practice Praying the Lord's Prayer

fight temptation, which leads to sin. Therefore, please give me this day my daily bread.

You forgave my sins by giving Jesus, Your only Son, to come and die on the cross for me. It was a sacrifice that He made. It is my human nature to return evil for evil. I pray Thee that You help me to forgive others for their wrongs so that You can also hear my prayer of forgiveness. Sometimes when I see the person who has hurt me, used me, and abused me, it brings pain to my heart. Without You, I cannot forgive them, Lord. I surrender to You that You will help me to forgive them their sins so that You will also forgive me of my sins.

Father, Your Word says that the steps of a righteous man are ordered by You and that I am the righteousness of God through Christ Jesus. I pray that You may lead me. With a willingness to let You have Your way in me, please lead me not into temptation but deliver me from evil. You are my deliverer. Without Your leading, some ways may seem right in my eye but only to lead me unto death. Help me, especially when I am with my peers, so that I may not go with the flow but be very conscious and make the right choices. Therefore, help me, oh Lord.

I surrender my life, my children, and my family to You. May You have Your way, for Yours is the kingdom, the power, and the glory forever and ever. Amen.

CONCLUSION

The Lord's Prayer has been with us for centuries. The Lord's Prayer was taught by the Lord Jesus Christ Himself. He was responding to a request that was presented to Him by His disciples to teach them to pray. The Lord then responded by telling them "to pray in this manner."

> Our father, who art in heaven, Hallowed be thy name, thy kingdom come, they will be done on earth as it is in heaven. given us this day our daily bread and forgive us our trespasses. lead us not into temptation but deliver us from evil. for thine is the kingdom, and the power and the glory, both now and forever more. Amen.

Jesus did not intend this prayer to just be recited, but it was meant to be used as a guide for the disciples to pray. The Lord's Prayer is like a skeleton that works well when there are tendons, ligaments, muscles, blood vessels, and all other components.

Coming into prayer with the realization of God as a Father to you, Jesus was establishing a relationship first before the disciples could ask for anything. With this understanding, they

– 69 –

The Secret and Power of Praying the Lord's Prayer

will not be afraid to go to God just as children are not afraid to ask their dad for anything. (under normal circumstances).

Let His name be hallowed in all you do, all you say, where you go. This is also true of the choices you make, either to do or not do. When overwhelmed, I have seen this work for me. When I did not know what to pray, I said as long as His name will be hallowed, I will be good with the results. At that time, that's all I could do because I felt like it was one of the darkest moments of my life. All I could hear within me was "hallowed be thy name."

Having His kingdom come and His will be done in our lives as it is done in heaven takes great total humility and surrender. This is because we humans were created with free will, and it takes humility to let another person's will be done and not ours. Letting His will to be done in our lives is overall for our good, for He has a good plan for each one of us, as recorded in the book of Jeremiah, chapter 29 and verse 11. Also, there are ways which may seem right in our eyes, but the end thereof are ways that lead to death. He is the only one who knows more about our tomorrow than we can remember of our yesterday. Let His kingdom come in your life, and let His will be done, not yours. Pray that your will may be in alignment with His will.

The Bible says that man cannot live by bread alone but by every word that comes out of the mouth of God. Jesus Christ is the Word that became flesh and dwelt among us. In one of His "I am" statements, He says that He is the bread of life. Therefore, asides from asking for our daily physical needs, let us ask for a daily portion of the Word of God through which we are to live. The daily portion of Jesus will give us the strength, the power to overcome sin, as well as build us up for His glory.

Once we see ourselves in the mirror of the Word of God, we will realize that we have all sinned and fallen short of God's

Practice Praying the Lord's Prayer

glory. As we desire to be forgiven, let us also forgive others for the wrongs they have done against us so that our Father in heaven may also forgive us our trespasses. For if we do not forgive others of their sins, our Father who art in heaven will not forgive us our sins. With God's help, we can forgive even those who we think do not deserve to be forgiven. God will give us the power both to do and to will for His good pleasure and for His glory.

The success of a family, team, or country depends on the kind of leadership in place. A good leader leads his team, country to greater heights. When the Lord is allowed to lead us, we are sure of our ending/landing. He will be with us all the way. A good leader leads to good places, not bad. Therefore, God leads us not into temptation but delivers us from evil because the kingdom, the power, and the glory are His both now and forever more. Amen and Amen.

ABOUT THE AUTHOR

Sarah Kerubo Nyandoro was born to the late Cleophas Nyandoro Onguti and Agnes Mauncho Nyandoro in Kenya. She is the eighth born in a family of fourteen children. Sarah knows what it means to have nothing and to have plenty due to her background. She grew up in a very poor family. Her parents were peasant farmers who struggled to have food to feed their large family, let alone tuition for their education in a country where tuition is paid for high school. In a family of fourteen children, the author had to struggle academically due to lack of school fees, and she also had to take care of her younger siblings as a house help, a responsibility taken by most girls growing up in her village at that time.

Sarah undertook her primary education at Nyamonaria and Machongo Primary Schools and passed highly in her Certificate of Primary Education (CPE). She then attended Nyamonyo Secondary School where she graduated with her Kenya Certificate of Secondary Education. Attending school was very erratic due to lack of school fees, but due to her cognitive grasp of educational content, teachers sometimes could retain her in school even when tuition was not paid.

She is a born-again Christian and believes in the power that there is in prayers and patience. She always said that her biggest inspiration was from the book of 1 Thessalonians 5:16–18, which says, "Rejoice always, pray without ceasing, in everything give thanks; for this is the will of God in Christ Jesus for you."

Sarah graduated from high school but could not join college due to the hardships of the family. She never gave up; she wanted to have a better life, and the only way back home was to attain a college degree. Ten years after graduating from high school, she joined Highridge Teachers Training College, where she became a primary school teacher. She was posted and taught in Kakamega County for a couple of years then moved to the US, where she resides now.

Her desire to become a nurse since she was in fifth grade was fulfilled when she joined and later graduated from Inver Hills Community College in the state of Minnesota USA with her Associate's degree in nursing. She later advanced her nursing career and obtained her Bachelor of Science degree in nursing (BSN) from Bethel University in Saint Paul, Minnesota USA.

Her love for the Word of God made her go to Spiritual Life Bible College and Seminary, where she graduated with her bachelor's degree in biblical and theological studies. If there is one thing to be remembered about Sarah, it is her resilience and never quitting. Sarah says that the challenges that she has gone through in life have drawn her to God and not away from Him.

She has the ability to hold on to her faith even when she does not see any way out.

Sarah works for one of the hospitals in the twin cities MN as a registered nurse. Sarah is also one of the associate ministers in the church she fellowships with. Sarah ministers to other groups both online and in person. Indeed, prayers and patience have helped a girl from a very humble background to attain her dreams and praise be to God. She now feels that writing is one of her newest passions, and what a better way to start her writing journey than to start with a book on prayer—not any other prayer but the prayer that the Lord Jesus taught His disciples to pray.

Sarah has been blessed with two children, Elizabethe and Jireh, who are the plight of her life. Both Sarah and her two lovely children reside in Woodbury, Minnesota. As she always said, do not despise small beginnings. It turned out that it is more applicable to her than she could have thought it to be.

Overall, Sarah is an extremely kindhearted person, who is always willing to help or listen to anyone in need. She's got a kind and gentle spirit. She is an excellent cook, and whenever possible, she spends time cooking for and with her kids. Her children call her the most thoughtful person they have ever met. She's always willing to go above and beyond for anyone. If she is able to help, she will even if that means sacrificing her sleep, time, or resources. Her heart is pure, so she is a blessing to anyone she comes in contact with, whether it's her family or a new friend!

CPSIA information can be obtained
at www.ICGtesting.com
Printed in the USA
BVHW081159090523
663838BV00006B/344